The Amateur
Navigator's Handbook

The Amateur Navigator's Handbook

Sallie Townsend
and
Virginia Ericson

Thomas Y. Crowell Company
NEW YORK   ESTABLISHED 1834

Designed by Ingrid Beckman

Manufactured in the United States of America

ISBN 0-690-00192-4

1   2   3   4   5   6   7   8   9   10

Library of Congress Cataloging in Publication Data

Townsend, Sallie.
      The amateur navigator's handbook.

      Bibliography: p.
      1. Navigation.   I. Ericson, Virginia, joint author.   II. Title.
VK555.T68 1974   623.89   73-15985
ISBN 0-690-00192-4

Acknowledgments

WE ARE GRATEFUL to many persons for sharing their knowledge with us, offering constructive advice, and giving freely of their time. It is, of course, impossible to cite everyone who has helped, but there are a few who deserve to be mentioned by name.

We have received most courteous service from the many government agencies we have contacted. Without exception, the men in these agencies have gone out of their way to furnish us with needed explanations and to supply us with relevant material. We particularly want to acknowledge the assistance of:

Mr. Oscar E. Arpin, New England District, United States Army Corps of Engineers, Waltham, Mass.

Mr. John Hanna, Public Affairs Officer, Lake Survey Center, National Oceanic and Atmospheric Administration, Detroit, Mich.

Mr. Vincent Kajunski and Mr. Gerard Sarno, Federal Communications Commission, Boston, Mass.

Mr. Robert Lynde, Marine Forecaster, National Weather Service, Boston, Mass.

Captain Philippe C. Gaucher, Chief, Boating Safety Division, First United States Coast Guard District, Boston, Mass.; and Lieutenant H. Roger Qualman.

We have relied heavily on the experience and advice of the technical members of our families: Sam Townsend, John Ericson and his brother William Ericson, Sam Townsend, Jr., and Lee Townsend. Cliché or not, without them this book could not have been written.

Many others have contributed in various ways to this effort. We are most grateful to past Commander of the Marblehead chapter of the United States Power Squadron Frederick Dike Mason for his help. He found no difficulty in understanding our objectives because of his years of experience in teaching the elementary piloting course, given by the local Power Squadron chapter, to beginners in boating.

George Quayle, past Executive Officer of our Power Squadron chapter and former instructor of celestial navigation, and Dr. Walter De Vries of the University of Michigan offered many excellent suggestions after reading an early draft of the manuscript.

William Konos (W. G. Konos Co., Beverly, Mass.), a competent specialist in marine electronics, and Richard Burns, an able engine and electronics technician, contributed information and advice in the field of electronics.

John and Joan Hooper, who are both sailors and airplane pilots, and Harvey White, owner and skipper of the 40-foot ocean racer *Whitecaps*, supplied us with some material and information on the Omnirange Direction Finding System.

Sound boating advice was given to us by George Berry, who qualifies as an expert by virtue of the long hours he spends, winter and summer, tending his lobster traps and fish nets in the waters off Marblehead, Mass.

Four friends in particular have spent many hours each as willing sounding boards for our ideas: Margaret Gerlach, Phyllis Hughes, Becky Seaver, and Lauretta Norris.

Fred L. Woods, Jr., owner of a nautical instruments store in Marblehead and an authorized chart agent, certainly qualifies as one of the most patient men in creation. We are constantly calling him for information on a variety of subjects, and he never fails us. To demonstrate his attention to detail, let us tell you about a "get well" card he sent to Sallie while she was in a nearby hospital.

The card read:

Dear Sallie:
  Lat.   42°30.4′N
  Long. 70°51.0′W
Is much nicer than
  Lat.   42°35.2′N
  Long. 70°54.3′W
Get Well Quick, and Hurry Back!
                    Fred L. Woods, Jr.

Contents

Foreword   xiii

Introduction   1

1 Cruising the Dining-Room Table   3
2 Information on Charts   12
3 Types of Charts   35
4 Ship's Compass   40
5 Plotting Courses   55
6 Speed and Distance Indicators   74
7 Ranges   82
8 Bearings   85
9 Danger Bearings   96
10 Fix   99
11 Running Fix   102
12 Circle of Distance   105
13 DR (Dead Reckoning) Track   111
14 Plotting Tacks—Power and Sail   115
15 Depth Sounding   125

16 RDF (Radio Direction Finder)   131
17 Radar, Loran, Omega, and Omni   143
18 Current   154
19 Leeway   164
20 Tides   166
21 Fog   170
22 Night Cruising   178
Appendix I   Publications   187
Appendix II Quick-Reference Lists   192
    A Chart Language   193
    B Plotting Procedures   200
    C Nautical and Statute Mileage Equivalents   207
    D Lights Carried on Boats Under Way   208
    E Fog Signals Given by Boats   210
    F Fog Signals from Navigational Aids   211
    G Right-of-Way   212
    H Distress Signals   215
Index   217

Illustrations

1 Parallel Rulers   8
2 Dividers   10
3 Dividers on Latitude Scale   30
4 True Course   58
5 Magnetic Course   58
6 Compass Course   59
7 Sample Course Line   66
8 Single Line of Position from a Range   84
9 One Bearing—Single Line of Position   88
10 Navigational Aid Abeam—Single Line of Position   93
11 Bow and Beam Bearing   95
12 Danger Bearing (example 1)   97
13 Danger Bearing (example 2)   98
14 Three-Bearing Fix   101
15 Running Fix on a Single Navigational Aid   104
16 Circle of Distance—Daylight   107
17 Circle of Distance—Night   110
18 DR Track   113

19 Tacking Under Power Compared with Following a
       Rhumb Line   118
20 Sailboat Beating to Windward (no current)   122
21 Dividing Rhumb Line and COGs by 4, Sailboat
       Beating to Windward (no current)   123
22 RDF Estimated Position   137
23 RDF Deviation Graph   138
24 Current 180° from Course   159
25 Current at Angle to Track   162
26 Lights for Power-Driven Boats of Less than 65 Feet   181
27 Lights for Sailboats Under Sail   181
28 Lights for Power-Driven Boats of Less than 26 Feet   182

Foreword

THE AMATEUR NAVIGATOR'S HANDBOOK provides a basic knowledge of coastal navigation in a form that is both practical and easy to understand. Written for the beginning boatman, the book is intended for use by the entire family.

The majority of boating accidents are due to ignorance. Since nearly forty-six million boatmen now navigate our waterways, safety on the water has become an increasingly important consideration of national safety. By furnishing the amateur boatman with a basic understanding of navigation techniques, the handbook makes an admirable contribution to the prevention of needless accidents that take such a large annual toll of our nation's human and economic resources.

By avoiding the confusion which many of the highly technical books on navigation create, THE AMATEUR NAVIGATOR'S HANDBOOK serves as a useful basic reference source. The handbook is to be highly commended for offering the beginning boatman a readable and valuable guide to safe, enjoyable boating.

A. C. WAGNER
Rear Admiral, U.S. Coast Guard
Chief, Office of Boating Safety

Introduction

WE BELIEVE STRONGLY that everyone over the age of twelve who steps aboard a boat should have some knowledge of coastal navigation, and the more the better. Not only is this an important safety measure, but the sport becomes more enjoyable and interesting as participation in this challenging facet of boating increases.

In this book, we cover many of the accepted techniques of navigation in a simplified and easy-to-learn format while making it possible still to achieve a high level of competence in the subject. Included are a number of backup suggestions of our own, learned from years of experience on the water.

We know from our experience that the more navigational techniques you have at your command and the more you use them, the better prepared you will be for all eventualities. Since it is difficult to retain all the details of navigational practice, we have included at the end of the book a number of quick-reference lists such as those we use on our own boats.

They will help you refresh your memory in a hurry about things you are likely to encounter most frequently while navigating aboard your boat.

1

Cruising the Dining-Room Table

WHETHER OR NOT YOU ALREADY OWN A BOAT, many fruitful hours can be spent "cruising the dining-room table" while you learn the mechanics of coastal navigation at home. This is the best and safest place to practice because you progress in the subject by actually planning and plotting sample cruises on a chart. With practice you will begin to develop into a competent navigator, ready to assume this responsibility aboard a boat.

Before we plunge into the subject of coastal navigation in detail, let's take a few pages to get any newcomers to navigation (or even boating) started so that they will have some basis on which to understand the following chapters. After all, the landlubber who wants to launch himself into boating is faced with not only a whole new concept of finding his way from Place A to Place B, but also a host of new terms to describe the process. If you already have a nodding acquaintance with boating terms, you can either skip this chapter or use it for a quick review.

Those of you who are really new to the water may not be familiar with the actual sizes and shapes of buoys, markers, and other navigational aids, which serve a purpose on the water comparable to that of traffic signs ashore. The best way to learn to recognize them is to buy or borrow a chart of your local waters and take it with you when you go aboard a friend's boat. (As you probably know, a map of the sea is always called a **chart**.) Ask your friend to show you the boat's location on the chart. Then, as you pass the navigational aids, try to spot them on your chart. Don't hesitate to ask for help; experienced boatmen usually show a missionary's zeal when newcomers ask for instruction.

As the boating trip from Marblehead, Massachusetts, to Gloucester is a logical first trip from our harbor, let's use it for a sample "dining-room cruise" to illustrate this simple plotting. To do this, we need nautical chart 1207 of Massachusetts Bay; part of an outdated edition of this chart is reproduced on the inside of the removable paper dust jacket of this book to illustrate explanations in the text and as a supplement for this chapter. Open out the sample chart on the table.

Charts, like 1207, which cover large areas do not show navigational features in harbors. However, the numbers of detailed harbor charts appear in parentheses in the plain blue-colored section of the harbor. (The different types of nautical charts as well as the government agencies responsible for their publication are described in chapter 3.) To simplify the plotting for this first cruise we are going to use only the large area chart, but in practice we would use harbor charts 240 and 233 as well.

Notice the many markings and symbols in the water areas—the white and blue portions of the chart. (Many of these are discussed in detail in chapter 2 and are listed in appendix II.) The little diamonds here and there mark the locations of buoys. At the tip of many of the navigational aid symbols on the chart is a dot that indicates the location of the aid; this is referred to as the **location dot**. A reddish-magenta circle over the location dot of a buoy symbol means that this particular navigational aid is lighted at night. (Hereafter in this book we refer to the magenta on the chart as "red.")

One of the main things to remember about the color of buoy symbols on a chart is that solid red is used for the red navigational aids that you are to keep on the right (starboard) side of the boat when entering a harbor ("red–right–returning from the sea"). The other solid-color symbol used is black: keep these buoys on the left (port) side of the boat when entering a harbor.

There is an old sea story about a captain of a large ocean liner who disappeared into his cabin at the same time every day and locked the door. This went on month after month, until the curiosity of the crew got out of hand. At their insistence the purser peeped into the captain's quarters and saw him open his safe and carefully remove a tattered piece of paper. At that moment, the captain was urgently called to the bridge and in his haste to leave dropped the mysterious piece of paper on a table. The purser seized this golden opportunity and, slipping inside, snatched up the paper.

Printed on it in bold letters were the words:

PORT IS LEFT

STARBOARD IS RIGHT

As a small boat is not likely to have a safe handy for a similar piece of paper, we suggest a memory jog for remembering which is the port and which the starboard side of the boat: " 'Port' and 'left' have the same number of letters, and both are shorter words than 'starboard' and 'right'."

To help keep this firmly in mind, the following is a review of four basic boating terms:

Bow: the front of the boat
Stern: the rear of the boat
Port: the left side, as you face the bow
Starboard: the right side, as you face the bow

Notice also on chart 1207 that the diamond of the lighted buoy symbol outside Marblehead Harbor is half red and half black. There is another one like it at the mouth of Gloucester Harbor. The two-color symbol indicates a junction buoy (see page 14). The word 'BELL' included in the description of the Marblehead Harbor buoy on the chart shows it is a type of sound buoy.

For the sample cruise, we'll plan a departure from the Marblehead red/black 'BELL' buoy and use the red/black buoy at Gloucester to enter that harbor. Look carefully at the chart to see if it is possible to go directly from one buoy to the other. The numbers printed on the chart between these buoys and elsewhere are **soundings,** indicating the depth (in feet) of the water at low tide. The soundings on this chart indicate that the water in the blue-colored areas is 18 feet or less in depth and the water in the white area over 18 feet deep. Therefore, the water is deep enough for your boat in any part of the white area; but it is necessary to check the soundings carefully while in the blue areas to be sure of enough depth. When a ruler is placed on the chart so that the straightedge intersects the location dots of the two buoys, it is immediately apparent that a straight-line course from the Marblehead buoy to the Gloucester buoy is out of the question. There are many places where the water is only 2 or 3 feet deep at low tide; and worse than that, you encounter '∗' or ' + ', symbols which mean there are rocks.

The best alternative then is to set a course for another buoy, and then go from it to the destination if this is possible. In this case, there is a lighted black 'WHISTLE' sound buoy in the white area just under the words 'Newcomb Ledge'. When the edge of the ruler is placed so that it intersects the location dots of the Marblehead 'BELL' buoy and the Newcomb Ledge 'WHISTLE' buoy, and then is moved so that it intersects the location dots of the Newcomb Ledge buoy and the Gloucester red/black buoy, it is apparent that there is plenty of water for such a course. Also, the solid-red buoy symbols between the 'BELL' and the 'WHISTLE' are on the correct (port) side of the course when leaving the harbor, and again correct as you are going in the opposite direction (red–right–returning).

Straight lines now can be drawn from one location dot to another: from the Marblehead 'BELL' buoy to the Newcomb Ledge 'WHISTLE' buoy, and from the 'WHISTLE' buoy to the Gloucester red/black buoy. These lines are called **course lines**. For accuracy, a sharp pencil should always be used for drawing on charts.

While a straightedge ruler may be used to draw a course line, a navigator is likely to use **parallel rulers** instead. This instrument (available from nautical or engineering supply stores) consists of two rulers connected in such a way that they may move independently of each other while remaining parallel.

It is possible to draw a course line with the parallel rulers and then find its direction in degrees, by "walking" the rulers across the chart to the nearest **compass rose**—a large double circle of numbers with a star at the top. (A compass rose is printed on the left-hand side of the sample chart.)

Once the course line is drawn with one edge of the rulers, press down firmly on that ruler and move the other one in the direction of the nearest compass rose. Press down firmly on the second ruler while the first is moved carefully into a closed position next to it. Repeat the process, continuing to "walk" the rulers until one edge intersects the exact center of the positioning mark, or ' + ', in the center of the compass rose and extends into the circles of numbers around it. (One drawback in using parallel rulers is the possibility of slippage; unless *firm pressure* is applied on one ruler or the other when you "walk" them, you may lose your place and have to start all over again.) The direction of this course line is read from the compass rose. As most compasses on pleasure boats are magnetic, we will for now disregard the outer circle of true degrees. It is important that you use only the magnetic degrees of this course, which are found on the inner circle. The longer lines in each of the

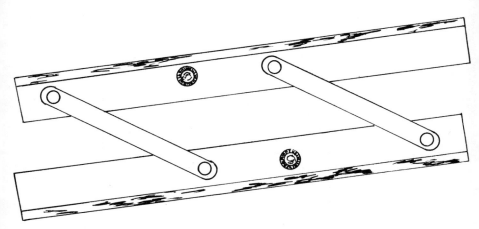

Fig. 1. Parallel rulers.

compass rose circles are ten degrees apart.

Read along the edge of the parallel ruler in the direction of the course; you will find it passes through 102° on the magnetic (inner) circle of the compass rose. Write the direction '102°' on the chart and follow it by the abbreviation 'MAG' (for "magnetic"), above the course line. Repeat this process from the Newcomb Ledge 'WHISTLE' buoy to the red/black buoy in Gloucester Harbor to find the number of magnetic degrees for your second course.

If you were aboard your boat, you would now steer from the Marblehead 'BELL' buoy to the Newcomb Ledge 'WHISTLE' buoy by following a compass course of 102°. Then, the compass course from the 'WHISTLE' buoy to the red/black buoy in Gloucester Harbor would be 047° MAG.

By steering carefully from the 'BELL' buoy, you would arrive at the 'WHISTLE' buoy provided there was no current and your compass was correct. Since the certainty of your arrival, as planned, at the 'WHISTLE' buoy is subject to these qualifications, we suggest you make only short trips in very good weather until you have studied further. For example, correcting for errors in the compass opens a whole new bag of tricks related to the term **deviation**. To understand this, you must read chapter 4; here, among other things, you will learn the "True Virgins Conversion Steps," which, we regret to point out, have to do only with mathematical figures.

The time it will take to make a trip is important, particularly since you do not want to be caught out after dark until you have more experience on the water. In order to figure this out, it is necessary to find the distances of the two course lines. **Distance** in nautical miles is usually measured by using the scales on the sides of the chart; these are called **latitude scales** and are discussed in chapter 2. For now, use the 'Nautical Miles' scale at the top of this chart.

Customarily, **dividers** (which may be purchased at nautical or engineering supply stores) are used to measure the lengths of the course lines and then to find their distances on a mileage scale. Dividers have two legs terminating with sharp points. They are joined at the top with a pin so that the legs can be separated to adjust for different measurements.

The points are placed on the chart, one on each end of the measurement you wish to determine; in this case, place them on the location dots of the buoys at each end of one course line. Hold the dividers carefully in this position, lift them, and place one point on the 'Nautical Miles' scale; wherever the second point falls on the scale is the distance. Repeat the process for the second course line and write the mileage figures (followed by the abbreviation 'MI' for "miles") above the course lines. Tenths of miles are written after a decimal point. You will, therefore, have '3.5 MI' for the course line from the Marblehead 'BELL' buoy to the Newcomb Ledge 'WHISTLE' buoy, and '5.2 MI' from the Newcomb Ledge 'WHISTLE' to the Gloucester red/black buoy.

The second piece of information necessary for figuring how long it will take to make the trip is the cruising **speed** of your boat. If you have a speed indicator aboard, this is no problem. However, if you do not have one, there are other methods by which speed can be determined; these are detailed in chapter 6. The speed is written *under* the course lines on the chart,

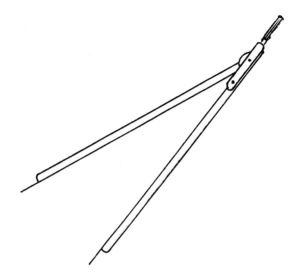

Fig. 2. Dividers.

preceded by capital 'S' (for "speed"). Here we will assume it is 8 knots and write 'S 8' under both the course lines. A **knot** in nautical lingo means a nautical mile per hour—the whole thing—so it is incorrect to say "knots per hour" as you would when referring to statute miles on land. (A nautical mile equals 1.15 statute miles.)

Once the distances of the courses and the average cruising speed of the boat are known, you can figure out the **time** it will take you to make the trip from Marblehead to Gloucester. Although there are **course calculators** (sold at most nautical supply stores) to help you do this, it is a matter of personal pride with us to do the simple arithmetic involved, poor as we are at math.

The known information is used in the **distance/speed/time formula,** or $60 \times D = S \times T$. Distance is calculated in nautical miles, Speed in knots, and Time in minutes. Whenever you know any two of these, you can figure out the third by using this formula or a variation of it. Since our unknown is **time,** the formula used is this one:

$$T = \frac{D \times 60}{S}$$

It is good plotting practice always to figure the problems of each course in advance, and to make it a habit to follow the same format when doing calculations. We suggest writing the problem and the variation of the formula you will be using in a notebook. Then, substitute the known information into the formula, do the work, and underscore the answer with a double line. We have found that the routine of this format has stood us in good stead, especially when we were tired and more likely to make mistakes.

Problem:

Distance—3.5 miles
Speed   —8 knots
Time   —?

Formula:

$$T = \frac{D \times 60}{S}, \text{ thus: } T = \frac{3.5 \times 60}{8}, \text{ or}$$

(26.25) <u>26</u> minutes for the first course

Using the same method for the second course, you will find it should take 39 minutes—a total of 65 minutes for the cruise.

Let's review: You have now used a chart, parallel rulers, dividers, a sharp pencil, and a notebook. You have learned a few new nautical terms and know how to draw a course line on a chart; how to find the magnetic directions, in degrees, of your courses; and how to calculate the time it will take you to make the trip. There is, of course, a great deal more to navigating, but at least you have made a good start.

And now, welcome aboard!

2

Information on Charts

FAMILIARITY WITH THE LANGUAGE used on charts is basic to the study of coastal navigation. (For guidance in purchasing charts, see appendix I.) Chart language includes symbols, abbreviations, numbers, lines, colors, and scales, which impart a wealth of information to mariners. Since the use of only a few of these is explained in the notes on charts, it is very important to purchase *Nautical Chart Symbols and Abbreviations (Chart #1)* to have as a handy reference. The long list of translations in the "Index of Abbreviations" alone makes this low-priced investment worthwhile. This reference also includes explanations of sketches and words commonly found on nautical charts as well as colored illustrations of buoys and daybeacons.

Some of the basic usages of chart language are explained in detail in this chapter. The most common of these are listed in quick-reference list A.

Some of the symbols on charts identify many different types of buoys and beacons, which can be divided into four categories of sea signposts for boating. We discuss these categories from the viewpoint of a helmsman returning from the sea, either heading toward or planning to enter a harbor. The first category includes those aids which the helmsman keeps to starboard, or on the right side of the boat; the second category, those he keeps to port, or on the left side of the boat. The identification numbers on these aids increase in magnitude as he proceeds into a harbor from the sea. Included in the third category are junction markers; and in the fourth, midchannel markers. Often letters are painted on both of these types of aids for further identification, and the identifying letter is shown on charts inside quotation marks.

The black location dot adjacent to the symbol for a navigational aid represents either the actual location of a fixed aid or that of the anchor securing a floating aid.

Navigational Aids Kept to Starboard
(Returning from Sea)

Aids to navigation that a helmsman keeps on the starboard side of the boat are painted red, and this accounts for the old sealore memory aid "red–right–returning," to which we add for clarity "from the sea." Buoys to be kept to starboard are shown on the chart by a red diamond adjacent to the location dot. They are often identified by the letter 'N'. This letter indicates a conically shaped buoy called a **nun**—probably named after the shape of the headdress worn by some orders of nuns. The word 'BELL', 'GONG', or 'WHISTLE' used instead of the letter 'N' identifies a sound buoy.

Daybeacons are unlighted structures of various shapes and sizes. They are identified on the chart with a red triangle, and sometimes with the abbreviation 'Bn'.

When these navigational aids are numbered, even numbers are used. When they are lighted, the lights are usually red, although occasionally they are white. These lights can be fixed, flashing, occulting, or quick-flashing. (The abbreviations for light characteristics are explained on page 21.)

Navigational Aids Kept to Port
(Returning from Sea)

Aids to navigation that a helmsman keeps on the port side of the boat when returning from the sea usually are painted black, although daybeacons may be painted black-and-green or just green. Buoys to be kept to port are shown on charts by a black diamond adjacent to the location dot. They are sometimes identified by the letter 'C' (for "can") or with the word 'BELL', 'GONG', or 'WHISTLE' to indicate a sound buoy. A **can** is a cylindrically shaped buoy with a flat top. Daybeacons are identified with a black triangle, and sometimes with the letters 'Bn'.

When these navigational aids are numbered, odd numbers are used. Lighted buoys have green lights, although sometimes they are white. The light characteristic may be flashing, occulting, or quick-flashing.

Junction Markers

Junction markers include nuns, cans, bells, whistles, and daybeacons. The buoys are shown on charts by a diamond shape colored half red and half black—to indicate a buoy with red and black horizontal bands. (An example of a red/black buoy symbol can be seen on the sample chart at the entrance to Marblehead Harbor.)

A red/black horizontally banded buoy designates a junction or an obstruction. The color of the uppermost stripe on the buoy itself indicates the side on which the preferred channel is located; for this purpose, the buoy is treated as though it were entirely that color. These buoys are usually identified on charts with the letters 'RB' (for "red/black"). If there is also an 'N' or a 'C', the preferred side on which to keep the buoy is immediately apparent—nun buoys are kept to starboard and can buoys to port when returning from the sea. When some other type of buoy is used, the preferred side can be determined, other than visually, by finding the description of the buoy in the *Light List* (see appendix I). The color of the upper band will be listed first.

When red/black buoys are lighted, the light characteristic is identified on the chart by 'Qk Fl' (for "quick-flashing") or 'I Qk Fl' (for "interrupted quick-flashing"). The color of the light may be white, red, or green.

Midchannel Markers

Midchannel markers include nuns, cans, bells, whistles, and daybeacons. The buoys are shown on charts by an outlined diamond shape with a black line dividing it in half vertically—for a buoy with black and white vertical stripes. (Unfortunately there are no buoys of this type on the sample chart, but the symbol is illustrated in Fig. 4.)

Black/white vertically striped midchannel buoys designate a fairway or midchannel. When these buoys are lighted, the light characteristic is identified on the chart by either 'S–L' (for "short–long") or 'Mo (A)' (for "Morse code A," or . __); both of these mean that the lights have a short–long flashing characteristic. These lights are always white.

Daybeacons (Daymarks)

Daybeacons, or **daymarks,** are unlighted fixed markers attached to the ground beneath the water. They often mark a rock or shoal along the coast, or the confines of channel along a waterway.

Where symbolized on a chart by a triangle, the center of the triangle is the location of the daybeacon.

A helmsman leaves red daybeacons to the starboard side of the boat and black daybeacons to the port side when returning from the sea. Usually the triangle on the chart is colored either red or black; however, sometimes only the outline of the triangle is shown. Where this occurs, a careful study of the chart will help you to decide the wisest course to follow.

Colored illustrations of the many different types of day-marks are printed in the back of the *Light List* (see appendix I). Daymarks are important navigational aids in the Great Lakes and their connecting waterways as well as in the intracoastal waterways.

More than forty abbreviations are used to describe these structures where they appear in column 6 of the *Light List*. Interpretations of the abbreviations are given under "Standard Designation and Description of Daymarks" in the "General Information" chapter at the beginning of each volume.

Charted Ranges

Sometimes two or more structures, usually lighted, are so located that they may be visually aligned by a helmsman. Their purpose is to help him stay in a channel in a waterway or when entering a harbor. This arrangement of navigational aids is called a **range**. It is usually identified on a chart with the word 'RANGE' and with a dashed line connecting and extending beyond the navigational aids. A solid-line extension of this dashed line indicates the course a boat is to follow and the distance for which the range is to be used. (The dashed line is not to be considered part of the course.) Navigational aids used as ranges are designated in the *Light List* with the word "range" included in their descriptions.

Ranges in smaller harbors are not always government issue; sometimes the local residents are responsible for their placement. Fishermen in many parts of the country locate ranges with reflectors or lights for their own convenience at night. These are also of great help to the yachtsman. The caretakers on the lovely little island of Highborne Cay in the Bahamas, for instance, have placed two sets of ranges on the hillsides. One range guides visiting yachtsmen through the reefs at the harbor entrance, and the other leads them to a safe anchorage. The caretakers confess that the ranges were installed because they became tired of spending so much time dragging yachts off the reefs and sandbars.

Ranges are intended for use not only dead ahead but sometimes dead astern. This is especially true in intracoastal waterways, where many ranges are used.

Light List

Information given on charts for navigational aids is supplemented and amplified in the *Light List*. The *Light List* is published in several volumes in order to include all the navigational aids in the United States. Aids are listed in these volumes from north to south, and from east to west, in rivers, along waterways, in the Great Lakes, and along the Atlantic, Gulf, and Pacific coasts. An overall discussion of the general layout of the buoy system in the United States is found under the heading "Buoys" in the "Description and Use of Aids to Navigation" section in each volume.

The *Light List* is particularly helpful when you wish to find a detailed explanation of the light and fog-signal-sound characteristics of a navigational aid, or a description of a structure, such as a lighthouse, for visual identification.

Lighthouses

Lighthouses are permanent structures built on the mainland, on an island, or on a foundation which is attached to the bottom beneath the body of water. They are identified on charts either by a red teardrop symbol adjacent to the location dot of the structure or by a red circle superimposed on the location dot. Next to a lighthouse symbol, there are abbreviations and numbers to describe the color and particular sequence used for the light. This description is referred to as the **light characteristic.** Following this information is the **height** of the structure above the surface of the water at mean high tide and its **geographic range,** or the distance in nautical miles that the light can be seen at night by an observer whose eyes are 15 feet above the water. (On the Great Lakes, the geographic range is given in statute miles.) If the lighthouse also has a fog signal, the type of sound warning used is included in the description, such as 'HORN'. When the lighthouse has a radiobeacon as well, additional letters and symbols describe the beacon characteristics (see page 131).

Lightships (LS), which are anchored at specific locations off coastlines, serve the same functions as lighthouses and are labeled with the same type of information. They are identified on a chart with the drawing of a ship's hull; the location dot is a tiny circle at the base of the hull. Lightships are sometimes identified with the abbreviation 'LV' for light vessel.

Periodically, a lightship is taken off station for repairs and maintenance. It is replaced temporarily by a relief ship. Changes such as this are always reported in the *Local Notice to*

Mariners (see page 33) with a description of the relief ship and its sound and light characteristics, which are often different from those of the lightship it is replacing.

On the sample chart, next to the teardrop symbol for the lighthouse on Bakers Island, the description given is: 'Alt Fl W & R 15sec 111ft 16M' plus the word 'HORN'. Translated, this means the light characteristic for this lighthouse is an alternating, flashing white-and-red light sequence during a 15-second time cycle. This cycle is repeated continuously. The lighthouse is 111 feet above the water and its geographic range is 16 nautical miles. The type of fog-warning signal used is a horn.

More detailed information about light characteristics of this and other lighthouses appears in the *Light List*. The following information is taken from an old *Light List* and is pertinent to the information given on our sample chart. (You may not read the same information for this lighthouse on a newer chart or *Light List* because the Coast Guard makes changes to better the navigational aid system. Thus, it is always important to have up-to-date or corrected charts and a current volume of the *Light List*.) In this volume the reference number for Bakers Island light is given in column 1, and next to it, in column 2, the light characteristic is described as:

BAKERS ISLAND LIGHT
Alt. Fl. W. and R., 15^s
0.4^{s}W fl., 7.1^s ec.
0.4^{s}R fl., 7.1^s ec.

This detailed description of the light characteristic tells you that during each 15-second light cycle used at this lighthouse, there is a flash of white light for 0.4 second followed by an **eclipse** ("ec.") or dark period lasting for 7.1 seconds; then a flash of red light for 0.4 second and another eclipse for 7.1 seconds.

Additional information gives the specific location of this lighthouse "on the north part of island" and the physical description of the structure—"white conical tower"—which simplifies the navigator's job of spotting it in the daytime. The latitude and longitude of the lighthouse are also given (see page 27).

The *Light List* also explains the sound characteristic of the fog signal more fully: "HORN, diaphragm: 1 blast ev 30ˢ (3ˢbl)." This means that a diaphragm type of horn which sounds one 3-second blast every 30 seconds is used. The statement "Resident Personnel," which is included in the description of this lighthouse, has some bearing on the operation of the fog-warning signal here. According to the *Light List:*

  (a) Fog signals at stations where a continuous watch is maintained and indicated by the words "Resident Personnel" in column 2 of the lists after the name, are sounded when visibility decreases to 5 miles, and also whenever the fog whistle of a passing vessel is heard. . . .

  (b) Fog signals at locations where no continuous watch is maintained may not always be sounded promptly when fog conditions exist or may operate erratically due to mechanical difficulties.

  (c) Where fog signals are operated continuously on a seasonal basis or throughout the year, it is so stated in column 7 of the lists. . . .

As the names of lighthouses are not given on charts, it is sometimes difficult to find them in the *Light List*, where they are identified primarily by name. To find a lighthouse in these volumes, note from the chart the height of the structure above the water, turn to the section in the *Light List* covering the general area of its location, and scan down the right-hand side of column 6 under "Ht. above water" until you find the height figure for that lighthouse. If you cannot find a lighthouse in this general area section, do not give up. A few major lighthouses, such as the lighthouse on Eastern Point on the sample chart, are not listed in this section and appear only in the "Sea Coast" section in the front of the volume.

All the information given on charts for lighthouses can be used in many ways by a navigator. For example, the height-above-water figure can be used to determine your distance from the lighthouse in the daytime, and the geographic-range figure helps the navigator determine when he can first expect to see a light at night. The methods used to make these calculations are explained in chapter 12, "Circle of Distance."

Light Characteristics

Lighted navigational aids on charts are distinguished by red circles superimposed upon location dots, or by red teardrop symbols. Following is a list of the most common chart abbreviations for the light characteristics of lighted navigational aids. On charts these color and light sequence abbreviations are used in combination to describe many different light characteristics, but when a color symbol is not given on a chart for a lighted aid, the light is white. A detailed description of these combinations appears in the *Light List* for each lighted aid.

W   = white light—when this light is used on a buoy, the chart or the *Light List* will give further information about the light, if the light should be passed on a particular side.

R   = red light—when this light is used on a buoy it is to be kept on the starboard side of the boat when returning from the sea.

G   = green light—when this light is used on a buoy it is to be kept on the port side of the boat when returning from the sea.

E Int = equal interval—the lighted period is equal to the dark, or eclipsed, period.

F   = fixed—steady continuous light—may be white, red, or green in color.

Fl   = flashing—the light flashes at regular intervals, with the lighted periods shorter than the dark periods. It flashes no more than 30 times per minute. A flashing light can be used on lighted red or black buoys and may be white, red, or green in color.

Occ   = occulting—the light flashes at regular intervals, with the lighted periods equal to, or longer than, the dark periods. It can be used on lighted red or black buoys and may be white, red, or green in color.

Qk Fl = quick flashing—the light flashes 60 or more times in one minute. It may be white, red, or green in color and denotes caution should be exercised, as at a sharp turn of the channel.

I Qk Fl = interrupted quick flashing—quick flashes for about 4 seconds, followed by a dark period of about 4 seconds. It is used on red/black buoys. Caution should be exercised, for example, at a fork of a channel. At night, the color of the light indicates whether or not there is a preferred channel. If the light is red, the buoy is kept to starboard when returning from the sea; if the light is green, the buoy is kept to port when returning from the sea. If the light is white, there is no preferred channel.

S-L   = short-long—this is always a white light, with a short flash followed by a long flash. The sequence recurs about 8 times per minute. This type of light is always on a black/white

		midchannel buoy and may be passed close aboard on either side.
Mo (A)	=	Morse Code A, or dot-dash—light characteristics are the same as S-L.
Alt	=	alternating—a light that has a periodic change of color.
Gp	=	group—two or more flashing or occulting lights, with a noticeable dark period between the groups of flashes.
Sec	=	seconds—preceded by a number which indicates that the light will be seen once during the given number of seconds. For example, with a 4-second light, count 1 . . . 2 . . . 3 . . . seconds during the dark period; the light will appear on the fourth second.

Red sector—in the vicinity of some lighthouses there is an area on the chart called a red sector, which could be overlooked by someone with a sketchy knowledge of the meaning of chart symbols. The area covered by the **red sector** contains rocks, reefs, or shoals. You are alerted to this at night because the lighthouse beams a fixed red light over this danger area.

Directional light—sometimes a ray of white light is beamed from lighthouses to indicate a safe channel to follow at night. This ray, or sector, of white light may be either more brilliant within an arc of less intense white light or bounded on one side with a green light and on the other with a red light.

Dredged Channel Markings

When a channel has been dredged, it is marked on a chart with broken lines depicting the sides of the channel. The width and depth of the channel is usually printed inside these lines. Sometimes buoys and daybeacons lining a channel are located outside the edges, and therefore it is best to allow for this eventuality by leaving some sea room.

Soundings

The sounding figures printed on the charts are depth measurements for mean low water on the Atlantic and Gulf coasts; mean lower low water on the Pacific Coast; and a low water datum figure for the Great Lakes.

Mean low water is an average of all the low tides for an area; **lower low water** is an average of the lower of the daily low tides. In both cases, some low tides will be lower than the soundings on the charts.

The **low water datum** figure on Great Lakes charts should be compared with the latest *Great Lakes Pilot* and its supplements and with the *Local Notice to Mariners* (see appendix I) because of seasonal fluctuations in water depth.

A notation on each chart tells whether the soundings are in feet or fathoms, or, as on some of the Great Lakes charts, in both fathoms and feet, such as 3_2 (3 fathoms, 2 feet). (Six feet equal one fathom.)

Boatmen must be aware that continual changes in water depth may occur in areas with sand or mud bottoms, especially at the entrances to harbors, bays, and rivers which are exposed to strong currents.

Fathom Lines

Fathom lines on charts look something like contour lines on topographical maps, and in a way they can serve the same purpose because they show the different levels of the ocean floor. However, the boatman is more interested in the fact that these lines indicate uniform water depths in fathoms.

Several fathom lines are drawn on charts and they may be indicated with dashed, dotted, or solid lines. Chart 1 includes the symbols for most of the dashed and dotted lines. For example, on the sample chart the pattern '. . . . . .' of the fathom line bounding the blue area denotes a 3-fathom line, the line '. _ . _ . _' a 10-fathom line, and '_ . . _ . .' a 20-fathom line. A solid line will have the number for the fathoms written in the line, as '_____100_____'.

Along a coastline, the depth in fathoms of a fathom line can be determined by dividing 6 feet (there are 6 feet in 1 fathom) into the largest sounding figure just inside the line in question. Outlines are drawn around areas where depth figures are shallower than the waters within a specific fathom line.

As the blue area on charts is outlined by a fathom line, all soundings inside this line are shallower than those on the white portions of the chart. When a navigator is considering possible courses to draw on a chart, he is alerted to shoal areas by the blue coloring.

On harbor charts, the blue area usually indicates water depths of no more than 3 fathoms (18 feet), although sometimes sounding figures in the blue area of these charts indicate a depth of only 1 fathom (6 feet).

Heights

Heights for bridges and conspicuous objects like towers or lighthouses are given on the charts in feet above mean high water. Figures for mean high water are printed in the 'Tidal Information' table on some harbor and coast charts.

If it is necessary to go under a fixed or closed bridge in order to enter a harbor, you should know the vertical clearance required for your boat and compare it with the vertical clearance figure given on the chart at the location of the bridge.

If there is any question in your mind about the clearance, locate the time and height of high tide for that area in the *Tide Tables* (see appendix I) and the 'Mean High Water' figure for that location, or one nearby, in the 'Tidal Information' table. For example, if the 'Mean High Water' figure in the table is 8.7 for the area near the bridge (see the 'Mean High Water' figure given for Gloucester in the 'Tidal Information' table on the sample chart) and the high tide for the day in question, as determined from the *Tide Tables*, is 9.7, subtract 1 foot from the vertical clearance figure printed on the chart for any bridge near the harbor to determine its height above the water at high tide.

If your boat will just barely clear a bridge at high tide, it might be wise to wait until the tide is lower. Mute evidence of clearance *faux pas* is shown by the large dents in the CLEARANCE 55 FT. signs on both sides of the Thirty-Sixth Street Causeway fixed bridge in Biscayne Bay, Florida.

Compass Rose

A navigator can determine the direction in degrees of course and bearing lines from the compass roses printed on charts. On coast and harbor charts, each compass rose has two circles. True degrees are shown on the outer circle with a zero and a star at true north. Magnetic degrees (used with a magnetic ship's compass) are shown on the inner circle, the arrow at zero indicating magnetic north. The position of the arrow on the magnetic rose in relation to the zero at true north reflects the number of degrees of **variation** between the direction of magnetic north and the direction of true north. The variation ('VAR') is written inside each compass rose in degrees (°) and minutes ('). (There are 60 minutes in 1 degree.) As there may be differences in variation within the area covered by one chart, always use the compass rose nearest the location of your plotting.

Annual change in variation is also written inside the compass rose, but during one year this change is usually too small to have any significant effect on course directions taken from the magnetic rose.

For accuracy in reading degrees, make sure a navigator's instrument, such as parallel rulers, intersects the exact center of the positioning ' + ' located in the center of the compass rose. A straight line extended in any direction from the ' + ' in the center of the compass rose through the two circles, or roses, indicates both the magnetic and true degrees of that line.

Latitude and Longitude

A mariner on the trackless sea, out of sight of land- or seamarks, plots his courses on a chart by using **latitude** and **longitude**. Latitude and longitude are also used to describe the positions of navigational aids.

The coastal navigator uses this method of describing and finding locations in many ways: he corrects his charts by using the latitude and longitude included in each report of the *Local Notice to Mariners*, which lists hazards to navigation as well as changes indicated for navigational aids; he uses it to report his approximate position to the Coast Guard when he requires assistance; and he uses it to record his most probable position from time to time when he is away from land- or seamarks.

Lines drawn horizontally on globes, maps, and charts are called parallels of latitude and those drawn vertically are called meridians of longitude. These **meridians of longitude** are half-circles of equal length drawn on a globe from the North Pole to the South Pole, thereby dividing the globe into sections resembling those of a peeled orange. These curving lines, or meridians, are straightened out on coastal charts to become straight lines running from north to south.

The designation of each meridian is expressed according to its relationship to the **prime meridian,** 0° longitude, which extends from the North Pole to the South Pole through Greenwich, England. Although there are 360 meridians, one for each whole degree, they are divided into two groups of 180°. The meridians up to 180° east of Greenwich are referred to as **east longitude,** and the letter 'E' follows the degrees. Similarly, the meridians up to 180° west of Greenwich are **west longitude,** and the letter 'W' is used after the degrees. The 180° meridian is common to both groups, and does not need an 'E' or 'W' designation.

All the meridians running through the United States are west of the prime meridian; when longitude is written for this part of the world it is always followed by the letter 'W'.

The scales at the top and bottom of charts are called **longitude scales.** Designations, in degrees, of meridians drawn on each chart are marked on these scales. The '71°' in the top margin of the sample chart represents 71°W longitude, with the degrees increasing to the west.

Everyone is familiar with the **equator,** the imaginary line that divides the earth into the Northern and Southern hemispheres. The equator is 0° latitude, the North Pole 90°N (north) latitude, and the South Pole 90°S (south) latitude. Lines parallel to the equator are drawn around the globe and labeled from either 0° to 90°N or 0° to 90°S. These are called **parallels of latitude,** and the length of these lines become shorter and shorter as they near the poles. The scales on the sides of a chart are called **latitude scales,** such as '42°N' on the sample chart, with the degrees increasing to the north.

Degrees of latitude and longitude are divided into 60 **minutes** (′) so that a navigator can more precisely pinpoint a location on a chart. On both the latitude and longitude scales on the sample chart, each black and each white bar represents 1 minute. Each minute is divided into **tenths of minutes** by short black lines, with a longer line designating 0.5 minute.

To measure the degrees, minutes, and tenths of minutes, of latitude of a navigational aid on a chart, place one point of your dividers on the location dot of the aid and the other point on the nearest parallel of latitude directly above or below the aid. Holding the dividers carefully in this position, lift them and move them to the same parallel on the latitude scale on one side of the chart. Place one point of your dividers on this parallel of latitude. The degrees, minutes, and tenths of minutes, of latitude of the navigational aid are read from the nearest tenths-of-minutes line that the other point of the dividers reaches on the scale. A latitude of, for example, "forty-two degrees, thirty-one and two-tenths, north" is written: 'Lat. 42°31.2′N'. (See Fig. 3.)

Longitude is determined by using a similar procedure. The distance between the location dot of the navigational aid and the nearest meridian of longitude is measured with dividers. The dividers are then moved to the longitude scale on either the top or the bottom of the chart, and one point is placed on the same meridian of longitude. Where the other point falls on the scale is the longitude of the navigational aid.

Practice finding the latitude and longitude of navigational

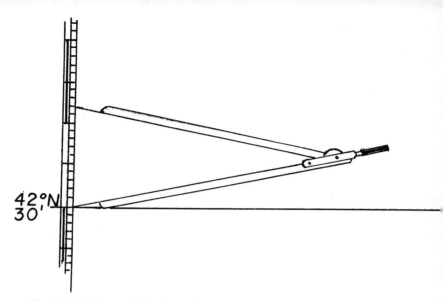

Fig. 3. Dividers on latitude scale.

Lat. 42°31.2′N.
    (Also a measurement of 1.2 nautical miles.)

aids on the sample chart. The location of one of the navigational aids on the sample chart, Bakers Island light, is 'Lat. 42°32.2′N', 'Long. 70°39.9′W'. Note on the sample chart the whole-degrees figure of '71°' marked on the margin. The minutes (′) to the right or east of this figure are for longitude 70°W.

Sometimes it is more accurate to measure latitude and longitude on a chart by placing the edge of a piece of paper on the location dot of the navigational aid and making a mark on the paper, and another mark where the edge of the paper intersects either a parallel of latitude or a meridian of longitude, depending on which you are using. The degrees, minutes, and tenths of minutes are indicated by the location of the marks on the edge of the paper where it is placed against the appropriate scale.

Distance in nautical miles is measured on the latitude scale:

    1 degree of latitude = 60 nautical miles
    1 minute of latitude = 1 nautical mile

Mileage for a course is usually figured to the nearest tenth of a mile by a navigator. On charts like the sample chart each black and each white bar on the latitude scale represents 1 mile, and each mile is divided into tenths. Points of dividers are placed at each end of a course line, then held carefully in this position and placed on the latitude scale. For example, the illustration of dividers on latitude '42°31.2'N' (Fig. 3) shows a measurement on the latitude scale of 1.2 nautical miles.

When a course line is too long for the spread of the dividers, open the dividers to a convenient measurement, such as 5 miles, on a latitude scale. Measure consecutive 5-mile segments of the course line, counting them as the dividers are pivoted carefully first on one point and then on the other along the course. Adjust the dividers to the remaining distance, measure this on the latitude scale, and add it to the number of 5-mile segments counted. (The longitude scales are used *only* for measuring the degrees and minutes of longitude and are *never* used for determining mileage.)

The majority of coastal charts are laid out in the **Mercator** system of projection. When this system is used, the parallels of latitude and the meridians of longitude are represented as straight lines. On Mercator charts, therefore, a straight line (called a **rhumb line**) can be drawn between two points on this round old world of ours, making it easier to plot courses and measure distances. Because the area covered on a Mercator chart has been artificially flattened out, the latitude scales have been adjusted to compensate for this, and thus the actual measurement of distances taken from them varies from one end of the scales to the other. For the greatest accuracy, particularly on charts which cover large areas, it is essential to measure mileage on the section of the scale nearest the latitude position of a course.

Systems of projections other than Mercator are used for many of the charts of the Great Lakes. The **polyconic** projection is the one most commonly used. In this projection, the meridians of longitude are not parallel as they are on a Mercator chart, although they may appear to be at first glance. The distance between two meridians will be greater at the bottom of a chart than at the top since the meridians converge toward the North Pole. The parallels of latitude on these charts curve up slightly.

When using polyconic charts, like those used for the Great Lakes, a navigator may handle the projection the same way he would a Mercator projection with the exception that statute miles are used instead of nautical miles. Distance is measured on the statute miles scale printed on these charts instead of on the latitude scales along the sides.

Coast Pilots and *Great Lakes Pilot* References

Often a note is printed on a chart that directs you to look up a description of a specific area in a *Coast Pilot* or the *Great Lakes Pilot* (see appendix I). These volumes, which are intended to be used with the charts, are extremely helpful to mariners because of the pertinent navigating information included in them. Although they are intended for commercial shipping, they are also of use for pleasure craft.

They include detailed descriptions of coastlines, harbors, islands, and port facilities, as well as rules and regulations governing the waters within the scope of each volume. They also give the locations of National Weather Service warning displays and Coast Guard stations as well as distance tables for the mileage between many harbors, and the merits and dangers of various courses.

Coast Pilots are published as eight volumes which cover the Atlantic, Gulf, Pacific, and Alaskan coasts. The *Great Lakes Pilot* includes six supplements which are issued from May through October during the boating season. The supplements are necessary because there are many changes in the Great Lakes' water depths during the year due to seasonal fluctuations, shoaling, and dredging.

These excellent references are published annually, and all boatmen who cruise should purchase and use the appropriate volume for their cruising area.

Local Notice to Mariners

Every boatman can call or write the office of the district commander of his local Coast Guard district to request that his name be put on the mailing list for the *Local Notice to Mariners*, which is published weekly throughout the year. This service is free of charge.

Reported in these issues are any changes in the locations of navigational aids as well as changes in the light or sound characteristics of buoys and lighthouses so that corrections can be made on the most recent edition of the chart in which they appear. Dangers to navigation, such as buoys which are off station, locations of wrecks, previously uncharted rocks, dredging operations, and times and dates of military firing exercises are also included.

No matter how recently a chart has been published, the boatman has a duty to himself and those who join him aboard his boat to keep his charts up to date. Continually correcting charts from these weekly notices may seem to be a tedious chore, but it is a sensible safety precaution.

The Coast Guard is constantly at work maintaining navigational aids and adding new ones as the need arises. It depends greatly on reports from boatmen to help in this tremendous undertaking. Often it is as a result of these reports that buoys which have been moved from their charted positions during storms or which have been damaged when they have been struck by boats are discovered and reported in the *Local Notice to Mariners.*

If you are planning to cruise in an area other than your home waters, you will have to correct the charts you will be using for these unfamiliar waters. An officer in the Aids to Navigation section of the Coast Guard district office in Boston advises you to write the Coast Guard district for the cruising area in question; request copies of their *Local Notice to Mariners* that have been issued after the publication date marked on the lower left-hand corner of the chart or charts you will be using. When a chart has been corrected rather than replaced by a new edition, a notification of this appears in parentheses following the original publication date on the chart, such as '(corr. thru N.M. 27/72)'. Translated, this means that the chart has been corrected for aids and hazards to navigation through *Local Notice to Mariners* Issue 27 of 1972. For subsequent chart corrections, you should order all issues published since Issue 27 of 1972. The Boston district office usually keeps back copies in stock for one year.

Not only are these weekly reports essential for chart corrections, but they are necessary so that you can keep your *Light List* up to date as well.

3

Types of Charts

THE NATIONAL OCEANIC AND ATMOSPHERIC ADMINISTRATION, a division of the Department of Commerce, is responsible for all nautical navigation charts in the United States. This administration hereafter will be referred to by its initials NOAA—pronounced "Noah" after the legendary Old Testament seafarer. Within NOAA, the National Ocean Survey is responsible for charts used for navigating along the coasts of the United States; the Lake Survey Center for charts used for navigating on the Great Lakes and the New York canals; and the U.S. Naval Oceanographic Office for charts of oceans, seas, and foreign waters.

Nautical charts may be sold only by persons authorized by the Department of Commerce. They are listed by geographical location in a pamphlet called *Authorized Chart Agents*; chart agents for the Great Lakes are listed in the *Nautical Chart Catalogs* (U.S. Lake Survey Chart Catalog) for the Great Lakes and connecting waterways (see appendix I).

You will need to have aboard charts of different scales for the same cruising areas, since the charts on which you plan your weekend or longer cruises are unlikely to include all the navigational aids at the entrances to or inside harbors.

For example, a scale of 1:40,000 means that one unit of

measurement on the chart represents 40,000 of the same units of measurement on the surface of the earth. In order to avoid excessively large-size charts, the scale, or ratio, must necessarily become smaller when larger areas of water and land are represented.

Harbor Charts

A small area of coastline is enlarged in detail on harbor charts, making them useful for entering harbors and anchoring. Because of the small area covered by a scale of 1:40,000, they are not practical for charting long courses.

Coast Charts

Coast charts, which are used primarily for planning and charting the day's run, are smaller-scale charts than harbor charts and are drawn to a ratio, or scale, of 1:50,000 up to 1:100,000. The sample chart, 1207, is an example of a coast chart and, as noted in its heading, is drawn to a scale of 1:80,000.

General Charts

These small-scale charts are used when the course is well offshore, and for plotting **RDF** (**radio direction finder**) bearings on distant radiobeacons. General charts are drawn to a ratio of 1:100,000 to 1:600,000. One general chart may be all that is necessary to cover your entire cruising area—1 foot of a 1:600,000 chart covers almost 100 nautical miles.

Although we plot most of our courses for weekend cruises on coast charts, we find the general charts particularly useful for drawing a course between buoys that are on different coast charts. Because it is difficult to line up two coast charts so that a course can be drawn accurately between these two buoys, it is much easier to draw the course on a smaller-scale general chart where both buoys appear on the same chart.

Compass roses on general charts do not include an inner circle showing magnetic degrees; therefore, variation figures given inside a rose must be applied to all courses or bearings taken from the circle of true degrees in order to use magnetic degrees (see "True Virgins Conversion Steps," page 44).

SC (Small-Craft) Charts

Inside routes, like intracoastal waterways and Long Island Sound, are charted on SC (small-craft) charts. True north is not necessarily at the top of these charts since they are often laid out to cover a curving waterway or coastline. There is at least one compass rose in each section of the chart, however, and there are also latitude and longitude lines drawn on them.

A notation on each chart indicates whether the degrees given for suggested routes or courses are true or magnetic degrees. Mileage figures along these courses are usually given in statute miles.

Great Lakes Charts

Sailing courses are already plotted between different locations on many Great Lakes charts. These courses are labeled

with true degrees, and the course distance is given in statute
miles. While the courses are intended for the convenience of
commercial shipping, the yachtsman finds them very helpful,
too.

Nautical Chart Catalogs

A list of all charts and their numbers appears in the *Nautical
Chart Catalogs* (see appendix I). In addition, an outline of each
chart is superimposed on the area it covers on a map of the
coastline and navigable waters. As there are many locations
where harbor charts, coast charts, and SC charts are available
for the same area, each is depicted in a different color for easy
identification. In the case of the Great Lakes catalogs, the
charts issued by the Canadian and United States governments
are represented by differently colored outlines.

Numbers and outlines of very small-scale charts used for
offshore or ocean navigation are shown in a separate section of
the coastal *Nautical Chart Catalogs* under "Sailing and General Charts." As an illustration of the scale of one of the sailing
charts, chart 1002 covers the area beginning just south of
Tampa, Florida, and includes Cuba and nearly all of the
Bahama Islands.

These catalogs are free of charge.

Volume 1 of the United States *Nautical Chart Catalogs*
covers "Atlantic and Gulf Coasts Including Puerto Rico and
the Virgin Islands," and Volume 2, "Pacific Coast Including
Hawaii, Guam and Samoa Islands."

The *Nautical Chart Catalogs* for the Great Lakes and
adjacent waterways can be obtained through either the U.S.
Lake Survey or the Canadian Hydrographic Service. (These
two organizations enjoy a close working relationship through-

out the whole area in addition to carrying on their independent activities on the four jointly bordered Great Lakes.)

If you tape the portion of the *Nautical Chart Catalogs* covering your cruising area near your chart storage place, you can refer to it quickly to find the numbers of the charts you will need for your day's run.

Date

You can find out the most recent publication date for a chart in the *Nautical Chart Catalogs.* When you purchase a chart, check the lower left margin for the date of issue.

4

Ship's Compass

ONCE YOU UNDERSTAND how to use a magnetic compass, your ship's compass becomes the most important navigational device aboard your boat. This understanding will make it possible for you to use a chart to its fullest potential. You will also be able to steer your boat to a distant destination with some assurance of arriving there even if you are out of sight of land or in an area with few navigational aids, or if there is poor visibility.

We feel that too many boatmen place an unwarranted amount of confidence in visual or "church steeple" navigation in which their total dependence is on actually seeing land- or seamarks. This type of navigation is adequate only when the weather is good and boating activity is carried on in a familiar area with either few navigational hazards or a number of buoys which are close together. However, even familiar landmarks and navigational aids disappear in a hurry during a sudden rain squall or in a pea-soup fog. When this occurs, it is essential to know how to find compass courses on your chart and to steer your boat according to these courses in order to reach a destination safely.

A classic example of an overconfident boatman piloting without a compass occurred one clear day on the Atlantic

Ocean twenty miles north of Boston. A large twin outboard cruiser roared up behind our boat and slowed alongside just long enough for the man at the wheel to shout, "Which way to Boston Lightship?"

"One, eight, zero degrees," our skipper called back, to which the questioner responded, "Don't bother with that, just point!"

The magnetic ship's compass, the type most commonly used aboard pleasure craft, has a bundle of magnetic needles attached to the underside of a compass card which is suspended in a fluid-filled bowl. The modern compass card is divided into 360° (000° to 359°) in a clockwise direction, with 000° (or 360°) indicating north, 090° indicating east, 180° indicating south, and 270° indicating west. This card pivots freely so that, in theory, the 000° on the compass card always points to a place on the earth of truly great magnetic attraction called the **magnetic North Pole**. The only time this might not occur is when metal objects on the boat itself exert some magnetic attraction on the compass or when the compass is in an area such as Lake Superior of the Great Lakes where ore deposits exert local magnetic influences. Both of these contingencies are discussed later in this chapter.

Three digits should be used in expressing direction when writing degrees on a chart, in a ship's log book, or expressing them verbally. Although you may hear degrees of a compass, such as 080°, expressed verbally as "zero eighty degrees" or even "eighty degrees," for sharp and clear communication it is best to say "zero eight zero degrees." By doing this, there is less possibility of misunderstanding, as in the case of a helmsman giving a compass course to a relief helmsman, or a helmsman shouting the ship's heading to a navigator.

In order to read the compass card and steer the boat on a compass course, it is necessary to have a fixed line of reference on the compass. This reference line is called a **lubber line** and is marked on the inside of the compass bowl. When the compass has been properly installed, an imaginary line drawn through the lubber line to the center of the compass card will be parallel to the **center line** of the boat, which runs from bow to stern down the exact middle of the boat. The compass reading for the **ship's heading,** or the direction in which the bow of the boat is pointing at any given time, is the degrees on the compass card which are in direct line with the lubber line.

Variation

The **geographic North Pole,** which is used as a reference point in drawing charts, is called **true north.** It is located at latitude 90°N, and it is here that all the longitude lines north of the equator converge. The **magnetic North Pole** is called **magnetic north** and is located about latitude 75°N and longitude 101°W. The difference between the attraction exerted by the magnetic North Pole on the direction of north as indicated by magnetic compasses and the actual direction of the geographic North Pole from various places on the earth's surface is called **variation.**

The problem of the amount of variation present in a particular area is solved for the navigator by the compass roses on coast and harbor charts. Not only is the local variation for an area written in the center of a compass rose but it is also demonstrated on the two circles of degrees by the location of true north on the outer circle and the location of magnetic north on the inner circle.

The amount of variation for a particular area, which is printed in the center of each compass rose, is followed by the letter 'E' or 'W' to indicate whether the location of magnetic north is east or west of true north. Slight differences can be noted even within the area covered by one chart, so be sure to use the compass rose nearest the location of your plotting for the greatest accuracy.

You will note on the compass rose on the sample chart that the variation is '15°30′W'. (The usual practice followed by most navigators on pleasure craft is to use the nearest whole degree when working with the figure for variation.) The annual change in variation on this compass rose is an increase of '1′ ' (one minute), and as mentioned earlier, it is too small to have any significant effect on course directions taken from this magnetic rose.

Local Magnetic Disturbance

In addition to the attraction exerted on a magnetic compass by the magnetic North Pole, there are a few localized magnetic fields on the earth which affect magnetic compasses near them. These are referred to as **local magnetic disturbances** and are noted on charts of the areas where they occur and in the *Coast Pilots* and *Great Lakes Pilot* (see appendix I). This condition is most likely to be encountered on some of the Great Lakes, especially on Lake Superior.

Deviation

Magnetic influences from metal objects located near a magnetic compass can alter the compass readings from proper magnetic readings. You can demonstrate this at home by placing a small compass on your dining-room table and then moving a metal object, such as a can or a bottle opener, toward it. Notice how the compass card on a ship's compass, or the needle on a compass with a fixed card, is attracted by the metal. The nearer the can is held to the compass, the greater the attraction.

The amount of change in degrees in the direction indicated by the compass while it is being affected by the can is called **deviation.** Thus, aboard a boat, the difference in degrees between the magnetic degrees of a course on a chart and the actual ship's compass reading for this course is also deviation.

A ship's compass can be affected by fixed metal objects such as the engine, electronic navigational instruments, and metal structural members aboard a boat. When deviation is caused by fixed objects such as these, it is possible either to compensate for the influence they have on the compass or to make up a table to show the amount of deviation present in the compass on different ship's headings.

The one thing you are unlikely to allow for, however, is the attraction exerted on the ship's compass by a carelessly placed metal tool or the like. Therefore, you must train yourself to be constantly alert to see that moveable metal objects are kept away from the compass.

The main thing to remember about deviation is that it is very personal to your boat. No other ship's compass is likely to have the same deviation as your ship's compass. Therefore, when we use the term *deviation,* we are using it only in its relationship to your compass aboard your boat.

"True Virgins Conversion Steps"

When both true and magnetic roses are given on a compass rose on a chart, it is a simple matter to find both the true and magnetic degrees of a course. As mentioned before, a straight line extended in any direction from the ' + ' in the center of a compass rose through both circles of numbers indicates both the magnetic and the true degrees of that line. However, on general or sailing charts, the compass roses have only the true rose; this makes it necessary to apply the **local variation** printed in the center of the rose to the *true* degrees of a course in order to find the *magnetic* degrees.

If your ship's compass is affected by *deviation,* the magnetic degrees of a course must be converted to your ship's *compass* reading by applying the deviation for that particular ship's heading.

The application of either variation or deviation, or both, to the degrees of a course on a chart is done very simply, by following the conversion steps explained below. Frederick Dike Mason, a loyal U.S. Power Squadron member and volunteer instructor of many classes in navigation, taught us the memory aid "True Virgins Make Dull Companions" to engrave on our memories the proper order to write down the first letters of *True, Variation, Magnetic, Deviation, Compass.* If you also remember "From true add west," you can find the compass course from true degrees by working down the steps in this order.

For example, assume the true direction of a course line, as determined from the compass rose on a chart, is 087°:

True	T True	087°	
Virgins	V Variation	15°W	(from compass rose)
Make	M Magnetic	102°MAG	("from true add west")
Dull	D Deviation	2°W	(from compass deviation table—page 47)
Companions C	Compass	104°C	("from true add west")

On the other hand, when you want to chart the true direction of a bearing you have taken, follow these steps in the *reverse* order because the information you start with is the compass direction of the bearing. Working up the steps from Compass to True, subtract west (this is explained on page 86).

In practice, most boatmen prefer to use magnetic degrees

from the magnetic circle on the compass rose to label their course lines drawn on charts and to use them for compass or steering courses. However, this is possible only if all the deviation error has been taken out of your ship's compass, because the amount the compass magnets are influenced by fixed metal objects aboard your boat changes according to the heading of your boat.

Compass Compensated by Compass Adjuster

A ship's compass can be adjusted to compensate for the influence exerted on it by fixed metal objects aboard a boat. It is possible to do it yourself if you have the equipment, but we have found it much more satisfactory and reliable to hire a professional compass adjuster to do the job.

An adjuster does this by determining deviation for different ship's headings and correcting any errors in the compass with adjustments to the magnets in the compass case as well as by placing magnets in different locations on the boat near the compass. If any small deviation error remains after he has made his adjustments, he will make up a deviation table which should thereafter be kept readily available aboard the boat.

On an auxiliary, the deviation of the compass may not be the same when the engine is being used as it is when the boat is under sail. Therefore, if the compass is compensated while the boat is under sail, the adjuster will have to repeat the whole operation with the boat under power in order to make up a deviation table to be used whenever the engine is running.

Rechecking the accuracy of the compass periodically by using the method described in the following discussion of deviation tables is necessary because adjustment magnets inside the compass case can slip out of place. Also, new equipment installed near the compass can affect its accuracy.

However, if you find errors in your compass, there is always a possibility they are caused by moveable objects inadvertently left near it. Sometimes the guilty party is just a beer can or a flashlight.

Once, while a bulkhead-mounted compass was being compensated on one of our boats, the adjuster removed a lampshade from a lamp on the bulkhead because it was in his way while he was working inside the back of the compass. Shortly after the adjuster left, the skipper, noticing the lampshade on the table, said, "Damn! I bet when this is put back on the lamp, it will affect the compass."

He sent the first mate to watch the compass while he replaced the lampshade. He was so right! The compass reading changed 2 degrees. We had to remove the lampshade whenever we were under way until the next time the compass was compensated.

Deviation Table

If you do not have your compass compensated to remove deviation error by someone qualified to do this, you will have to have a compass deviation table made up for your ship's compass before you can steer magnetic courses plotted on a chart with any accuracy.

You can do this yourself and it should have priority over many of the other tasks you have set for yourself aboard your boat. A deviation table is extremely important and should be used constantly by the navigator. Even a few degrees of compass error when you start to follow a course may mean that many hours later you have diverged unknowingly from this course by several miles.

As mentioned before, the amount the compass magnets are attracted by fixed metal objects aboard a boat changes according to the heading of the boat. Therefore, in order to make up your own ship's deviation table, you will have to compare your compass course for different ship's headings with magnetic courses you have drawn on your chart.

One method for making up a deviation table is to first plot on a chart several courses between various charted navigational aids. As determined from the inner circle of the compass rose, write the magnetic degrees of the course above each course line. If possible, these courses should be for every 15° of the magnetic compass rose, with at least one of the aids, such as a lighthouse, daybeacon, stack on shore, or the like, being in a fixed position. It is usually possible to have one navigational aid serve as a marker for several courses. For example, you may wish to set up the paper on which you will be jotting down your ship's compass readings for each course in the following way.

From Jones Ledge Daybeacon   Ship's Compass Reading

To Pine Island Light
To BELL 14
To Radio Tower WSSX

Other groups of courses could be set up in the same way. All of this preliminary work can be done at home.

Then, take your boat out on a calm day and at a time when there is little boat traffic to stir up the water. Position your boat so that the aids used for one of your charted courses are considerably ahead of you and you are able to line them up visually. Keep them in alignment as you steer your boat toward them and write down the direction in degrees of your ship's heading from your ship's compass. This is done for each course you have plotted. (When two navigational aids are used in this way to help a helmsman stay on a course more easily, they are called a **range**. Ranges are discussed in detail in chapter 7.)

A deviation table is made up from the magnetic degrees of the courses drawn on your chart and your ship's compass reading for the same courses. Section your paper into three columns.

In column 1, list the magnetic degrees of each course in order, starting with 000°. In column 3, write the ship's compass reading for the same course. In column 2, write the deviation (the difference between the magnetic and compass degrees). Add the letter 'W' (west) when compass readings are more than magnetic degrees, or the letter 'E' (east) when compass readings are less than magnetic degrees.

Your ship's compass deviation table might look like this.

Magnetic Degrees	Deviation	Ship's Compass Reading
000°	4°W	004°
015°	3°W	018°
030°	1°W	031°
045°	0°	045°
060°	1°E	059°

(etc. through 360°)

In the event that your magnetic bearing is not an even-15° number, you may estimate your deviation between the two given numbers or interpolate by formula, as shown on page 50.

The list of deviation figures on the table will usually increase gradually, once to the east and once to the west. Whether the deviation will increase first in an easterly or westerly direction will vary according to the individual compass. There will be no deviation in two areas of your table: once when the deviation changes from east to west, and again when it changes from west to east.

To use the table for steering a course:

1. Draw a course on a chart.

2. Determine the magnetic degrees of this course from the inner, or magnetic, rose of the compass rose on this chart.

3. Find these magnetic degrees in column 1 of the deviation table. Read across the table to the ship's compass reading and use this figure for the steering course of your boat.

If the magnetic degrees of a course do not appear on your table, average the deviation figures given for the magnetic degrees between which your course falls. Apply the averaged deviation figure to the magnetic degrees of your course to determine the degrees to use for steering. If you prefer, you can compute this intermediate value. This computation is called **interpolation,** which is explained below.

4. Write the compass degrees for your course above the course line drawn on the chart and follow it by the letter 'C' for compass. Using this designation each time eliminates the possibility of confusion.

Interpolation

When the degrees for a magnetic course drawn on the chart fall between the 15°-interval figures of the deviation table, it is possible to determine this course deviation by interpolation. Use the ship's compass deviation table given above to work out the following example.

Assume the magnetic degrees of the course are 021° and you wish to interpolate for the deviation. Set up two columns on a piece of paper, one headed 'Magnetic Degrees' and the other 'Deviation'.

In column 1, list the tabulated magnetic course degrees directly above and below 021° in the ship's compass deviation table. In this case, 015° is above and 030° is below. Fill in the magnetic course degrees, 021°, between them.

In column 2, write the tabulated deviation degrees given for 015° and 030°.

	Magnetic Degrees	Deviation
From deviation table	015°	3°W
Magnetic course	021°	?
From deviation table	030°	1°W

To make up the formula to interpolate for the deviation or magnetic course of 021° you need to determine the following.

1. The difference of your magnetic course from the tabulated magnetic degrees above it in the ship's compass deviation table. (Of course, it is also possible to use the magnetic degrees in the table that are greater than the magnetic course, but we prefer to do it this way.)

$$\begin{array}{ll} 021° & \text{your course} \\ -015° & \text{course above} \\ \hline 6° = & \text{difference in tabulated course and your course} \end{array}$$

2. The difference, or the **spread,** between the magnetic degrees used in the ship's compass deviation table.

$$\begin{array}{l} 030° \\ -015° \\ \hline 15° = \text{spread} \end{array}$$

3. The difference between the actual deviation figures used in the ship's compass deviation table.

$$\begin{array}{l} 3°W \\ -1°W \\ \hline 2°W = \text{tabulated deviation difference} \end{array}$$

The following formula is then used.

$$\frac{\text{Difference in tabulated course and your course} \times \text{Tabulated deviation difference}}{\text{Spread}}$$

Round off the answer to the nearest degree; thus,

$$\frac{6° \times 2°}{15°} = \frac{12°}{15°} = 1°$$

The answer to this formula is then applied as below to the deviation figure from the ship's compass deviation table. (The decision to subtract or add the product of the formula is reached by inspection of the deviation degrees taken from the ship's compass deviation table. The interpolated deviation degrees for the magnetic course in question must fall between the tabulated deviation degrees, that is, between 1°W and 3°W in this example.)

$$
\begin{array}{r}
3°W \\
-1° \\
\hline
2°W
\end{array}
= \text{deviation for a magnetic course of } 021°
$$

The completed interpolation table for magnetic course 021° follows.

	Magnetic Degrees	Deviation
From deviation table	015°	3°W
Magnetic course	021°	2°W (answer)
From deviation table	030°	1°W

Emergency Compass

If anything should happen to the ship's compass, a **hand-bearing compass** can be used instead. In order to have it serve as a reliable back-up compass, should the necessity arise, a position should be predetermined where it can be mounted. A deviation table can be made up for the handbearing compass, when it is in this position, by taking readings for every 15°

from the compensated ship's compass and comparing these readings with the readings taken for the same ship's headings on the handbearing compass.

A handbearing compass can also be used for taking bearings on navigational aids, landmarks, and other boats. This is discussed in chapter 8, "Bearings."

Digital Read-Out Compass

A magnetic ship's compass which features a separate screen unit on which the compass heading is presented in numerals is also manufactured. This is called a **digital read-out compass.** There are also remote units available which repeat the digits flashed on the main read-out screen.

This system is convenient for navigating because the navigator can read the ship's heading instantly, as it is flashed on the main display unit. This unit can be placed in a location some distance from the compass.

One of the features of this system is that *variation* can often be manually set into this type of compass. (Remember, however, that variation can be different even within the confines of one chart as shown by the compass roses, and you must reset the compass accordingly as changes in variation occur while cruising from one area to another.) If your compass has been compensated for *deviation,* the ship's compass reading will be a *true* heading.

As a safeguard, there should be a reliable conventional compass aboard in case of a malfunction in the digital read-out type.

Compass Direction to Identify Shoreline

Occasionally compass directions can be used to compare actual shoreline changes with the shoreline on your chart to discover your position along it. Sometimes this is necessary when you have made a landfall while cruising in unfamiliar waters and discover unbroken shoreline ahead instead of the anticipated harbor entrance.

The Townsends found this very helpful on their initial approach to Eleuthera Island in the Bahamas when heading for the entrance to Hatchet Bay. The Bahama Islands have a scarcity of navigational aids, and the entrance to Hatchet Bay is obscure to say the least.

When they first sighted Eleuthera, they saw sheer gray cliffs running for miles in either direction. There was no sign of the entrance to Hatchet Bay, described as "an artificial cut through limestone cliffs." It was difficult to figure out which twin white silos the *Yachtsman's Guide to the Bahamas* referred to as a guide to the entrance, since there were so many dotting the landscape.

The direction of Hatchet Bay from their landfall depended on whether they had over- or underestimated the speed of the current. While studying the chart and scanning the shore for a hint of their location, the skipper noted that the shoreline on the chart angled off in a noticeable change of direction at Hatchet Bay. He changed his course to parallel the shore, calling off the compass direction, which was compared to the chart. By this method, they discovered the harbor to be to starboard of their initial approach to the island.

5

Plotting Courses

ONE LABELING SYSTEM IS GENERALLY ACCEPTED by most navigators when plotting on charts, although occasionally there will be slight variations in the use of terms. Careful navigators always clearly label any changes they make from the accepted format.

This custom of using one system and labeling any changes from it is done with good reason. It makes it possible for others aboard to relieve the navigator from time to time and to check his work should he request it. This is particularly important when courses have been plotted under difficult conditions, such as during a storm, or when the navigator is tired. Both of these are times when anyone is most likely to make mistakes.

When working navigational problems, we write them down in a notebook used exclusively for all our calculations, do the calculations, and underline the solutions with a double line. These solutions are used in our plotting on charts and sometimes are entered in the ship's log book. If we have to recheck our calculations, this permanent record of our work is at hand.

We use *magnetic degrees* in most of our discussions and examples of plotting even though it is customary in many coastal navigation courses to teach students to use true

degrees. Most navigators aboard pleasure craft have a magnetic ship's compass and therefore find it simpler and quicker
to use magnetic degrees taken from the inner, or magnetic,
rose of a compass rose on a chart for course directions. In
addition, if their ship's compass has been compensated for
deviation, course degrees taken from the magnetic rose can be
used for a compass or steering course. Thus, the need for using
the "True Virgins Conversion Steps" is eliminated. Since this is
what is done in actual practice aboard pleasure boats, we feel
it is sensible for beginners to learn to plot this way from the
start.

However, there are times when the direction of courses
should be expressed in true degrees, such as in an emergency
when you report your course over your radiotelephone. Large
ships and Coast Guard vessels, which hopefully will pick up
your distress signal and come to your assistance, use gyro
compasses and these compasses tend to indicate true north.

True degrees are also often used when plotting is done on
small-scale (offshore) charts—compass roses on most of these
charts do not include a circle of magnetic degrees or a
magnetic rose. The local variation is written inside the circle of
true degrees, and the true degrees must be converted to a
compass course to be meaningful to a helmsman who is
steering by a magnetic ship's compass.

As you may remember, it is a simple matter to find the true
degrees of a course when you know the magnetic degrees on
compass roses that have both true and magnetic roses. A
straightedge placed across a compass rose on the inner-circle
magnetic degrees of your course will intersect the true degrees
of this course on the outer circle.

Course Line

You already know that a straight line drawn on a chart to indicate the track you wish to follow to a destination is called a **course line**. The direction in degrees of a course line on a chart is determined from the compass rose nearest to your plotting. These degrees are always written above the course line that you have drawn on a chart and are preceded by the letter 'C' for course. When a course direction falls between two degrees, a navigator generally uses the nearest whole degree figure.

Course lines can be drawn on polyconic charts, such as those used for the Great Lakes, just as they are drawn on the Mercator charts used for coastal areas. Course directions in both cases are taken from the compass rose nearest to the plotting.

True, Magnetic, and Compass Degrees

The same course line can be labeled in three different ways:

1. When the degrees of a course are not followed by either an abbreviation or a letter, these degrees are assumed to be true degrees. For example, a true course of 090° would be labeled as in Fig. 4.

2. To avoid confusion, we always label magnetic degrees with the abbreviation 'MAG'. Magnetic degrees are used in most of our discussions and examples of plotting. (See Fig. 5.)

3. When a ship's compass has not been compensated, we suggest applying the deviation from your deviation table to the magnetic degrees of the course so that you

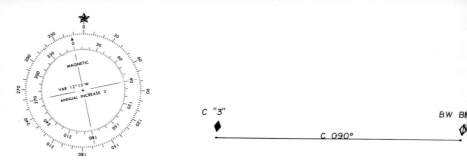

Fig. 4. True course.

Course: 090° true from 'C "3" ' to 'BW BELL'.

The outer circle of numbers in the compass rose is used. These true degrees cannot be used for steering a compass course until:

a) variation figures from the center of the rose have been applied (090° + 12° = 102° magnetic).

b) deviation from the ship's compass deviation table has been applied to the magnetic reading if the compass has not been compensated.

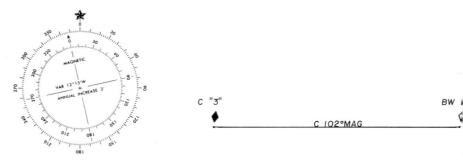

Fig. 5. Magnetic course.

Course: 102° magnetic from 'C "3" ' to 'BW BELL'.

The inner circle of numbers in the compass rose is used. These magnetic degrees can be used for steering a compass course if the compass has been compensated. If the compass has not been compensated, the deviation from the ship's compass deviation table must be applied to the magnetic reading.

can write your compass degrees above the course line you have drawn on a chart. The degrees of this compass course should be *followed by* the letter 'C' for "compass."

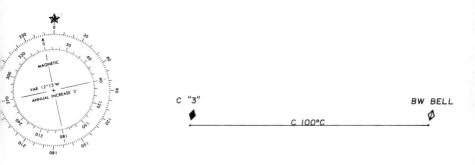

Fig. 6. Compass course.

Course: 100° compass from 'C "3"' to 'BW BELL'.
  (This assumes that a deviation of 2°E has been ascertained from the ship's compass deviation table and applied to the magnetic course of 102°.)

Distance (Mileage)

Frequently the course mileage, or the distance between two navigational aids, is written above a course line and followed by the abbreviation 'MI' for miles. Most navigators carry their mileage figure to tenths. The distance in nautical miles and tenths of miles is measured with dividers. This distance is taken to one of the latitude scales along the side of the chart where 1 minute of latitude equals 1 nautical mile. (This method is illustrated in Fig. 3.) Distance can also be measured on distance scales, which are printed on coastal charts. It is always measured on this scale on polyconic charts such as those used for the Great Lakes.

Sometimes the distance to be measured is too long for a single extension of the dividers. When this happens, extend the dividers to a convenient latitude-scale measurement, such as 5 miles on a 1200 series chart like the sample chart. Place one point of the dividers on one end of the distance to be measured and the other point where it would land, in this case, 5 miles along the course. Pivot the dividers on the point of the second leg and make the next 5-mile measurement. Continue to do

this, totaling the 5-mile segments as you go, until the last part
to be measured is less than the 5-mile extension of the dividers.
Then, close the dividers enough to measure the distance
remaining. Take the dividers to the latitude scale for this
shorter measurement and add it to your last total for your final
answer.

Mileage figures for distances are often given on inland
charts. Sometimes mileage is determined from the start of a
particular waterway, as on intracoastal (SC) charts and
Mississippi River charts; other times it is given for suggested
sailing courses printed on charts such as those for the Great
Lakes.

On inland charts, mileage figures usually are given in statute
or land miles. If mileage figures are given in nautical miles, a
notation of this is printed somewhere on the chart. Canadian
charts of the Great Lakes often give mileage distances of
sailing courses in statute miles, with nautical miles in parentheses.

A statute mile is 5,280 feet in length. A nautical mile is 1.15
statute miles and is 6,076 feet long. The nautical mile was
originally adopted for navigation because it is equal to 1
minute of latitude.

When your boat speed indicator registers in knots (which
are nautical miles per hour) and the distance figures on your
chart are given in statute miles, either speed or distance has to
be converted so that both are expressed in the same unit of
measurement.

The conversion table for nautical and statute miles is given
in quick-reference list C.

Speed

The speed at which a boat moves through the water is
referred to as **boat speed;** it is recorded underneath a course

line and preceded by the letter 'S' for speed.

Aboard a boat, speed is customarily registered in knots. (As you already know, the definition of knots includes both distance and time.) A boat moving at a steady speed of 6 knots for a period of one hour probably has not covered a distance equal to 6 nautical miles over the ground, and therefore it has not achieved the actual distance of 6 statute miles an automobile traveling at 6 miles per hour for one hour would cover on land. The boat speed refers only to the boat's movement through the water; there are many other influences, such as wind, waves, and current, affecting its overall progress.

Twenty-Four–Hour Time

Time is expressed aboard a boat by using the full twenty-four hours of a day instead of using two twelve-hour segments and labeling them A.M. and P.M. In twenty-four–hour time, midnight is '2400' for the old day, and '0000' for the new day, with noon expressed as '1200'. (When converting watch time to twenty-four–hour time, it may help to remember, "after noon, add twelve.") Thus, 2:30 P.M. is written on the chart or in the ship's log book as '1430'.

It is essential to learn to think of time this way because it is used in navigational reference books such as the *Tide Tables* and the *Tidal Current Tables* (see appendix I). It is also convenient to use when figuring out plotting problems such as the time it will take a boat to travel a particular course in order to estimate its time of arrival at a buoy or the like. In addition, if you have a radiotelephone aboard your boat, the Federal Communications Commission states that "the 24 hour system is used in a radio log."

When you are working with twenty-four–hour time, the first two digits are hours and the last two digits are minutes. To avoid possible errors when you add or subtract these figures, place an 'ʰ' after the hour digits and an 'ᵐ' after the minute digits; thus, 2141 hours is written as '21ʰ41ᵐ'. This serves as a reminder that 60 is the unit used in the minute column. For example, to add 50 minutes to 2141 hours:

$$21^h41^m$$
$$+\quad 50^m$$
$$22^h31^m \text{ (the minutes total 91, or 1 hour and 31 minutes)}$$

Sometimes, before subtracting one time from another time, the number on the upper line must be changed by subtracting 1 hour and adding 60 minutes. For example, subtract 50 minutes from 2231 hours:

$$22^h31^m =\quad 21^h91^m \text{ (one of the hours is converted to}$$
$$-\quad 50^m\quad -\quad 50^m\quad \text{minutes)}$$
$$21^h41^m$$

For clarity, twenty-four–hour time should be written and expressed verbally in four digits. For example, half past six in the morning is written '0630' and expressed verbally as "zero six three zero." The even hour is often referred to casually as "zero six hundred," but it is better to say all the zeros for sharp and clear communication as is done on marine and aviation broadcasts.

A clock or wrist watch with a second hand is essential for coastal navigation. Unless you plan to do celestial navigation, a precision timepiece or chronometer is not necessary.

Distance/Speed/Time Formula

The formula

$$D = \frac{S \times T}{60}$$

is used to calculate the *Distance* in nautical miles from the boat *Speed* in knots and *Time* in minutes. This multipurpose formula is affectionately referred to by boatmen as "Sixty D Street." This memory aid arises from another way of writing it, which is $60D = ST$. If your algebra is weak, just memorize the following three uses of the formula or jot them down on the first page of your ship's log book as we do.

Distance:

$$D = \frac{S \times T}{60}$$

Speed:

$$S = \frac{D \times 60}{T}$$

Time:

$$T = \frac{D \times 60}{S}$$

Course calculators which help you solve distance, speed, and time problems are available at many marine supply stores.

Plotting a Course Line

When plotting a course line on a chart, choose a known position as a starting point and another as a destination. Check for charted hazards along the way, such as ' + ' and ' $*$ ', which show rocks, and those sounding figures which indicate shoal water. We circle hazards near the course in pencil to remind us of their presence.

When a course is between two buoys, the line is drawn from the location dot of the first buoy to the location dot of the second buoy. The straight line of a course can be drawn with parallel rulers, which are then walked to the compass rose and placed on the positioning ' + ' in the center. The magnetic degrees of the course are read from the inner numbered circle. When a particularly long straight line is necessary, a gas tank measuring stick, a sail batten, or even the edge of a chart can be used to draw the course line.

The magnetic degrees of the course are written near the starting point. When we plan to use the same course line for a return trip, we record the reciprocal of the course direction by adding or subtracting 180° and we mark this on the course line near the destination buoy. You may wish to further identify course directions with arrows.

When the boat is under power, the anticipated speed is recorded below the line. Boat speed must be estimated for boats under sail because the speed will vary according to changes in the strength of the wind, but it is recorded the same way.

The distance of the course is measured and the mileage is recorded above the course line. The time the starting buoy is passed close aboard is noted on the chart or in the ship's log book.

An ETA (estimated time of arrival) at the destination buoy can be determined by using the distance/speed/time formula

$$T = \frac{D \times 60}{S}$$

and adding the answer to the time the starting buoy was passed close aboard.

For an example of ETA, assume 'C "3" ' is passed close aboard at 10:32 A.M., or '1032'. The speed of the boat is 6 knots. The mileage or distance of the course is 6.2 miles to 'BW BELL'.

$$\frac{D \times 60}{S} = T; \quad \frac{6.2 \times 60}{6} = 62 \text{ minutes}$$

$$10^h 32^m$$
$$+ \quad 62^m$$
$$11^h 34^m$$ or 11:34 A.M. is the ETA at 'BW BELL'

This course line might be drawn and labeled as shown in Fig. 7.

Plotting a Day's Run

Many cruising families prefer to do the chart work for a weekend cruise on the dining-room table prior to the cruise. At this time, the whole family discusses where they would like to go each day. Once a decision is made, the course lines are drawn from buoy to buoy on the charts, with notations of their magnetic degrees, the distances between buoys, and if the family boat uses power alone, the cruising speed they expect to maintain. By doing this, the entire family participates in the planning for a cruise and the younger members learn to navigate.

Our friends Edward and Barbara Woll have devised a very workable card file for courses from their home port to many other ports. The cards are titled with the destination harbor and filed alphabetically. The information on each card includes the number (or numbers) of the charts used, the total mileage and time for both the fair weather route and the alternate route (discussed below), and the cruising speed used to figure the running times. When they are cruising, they use this efficient card file system but always have the charts aboard which they have used to make up the cards.

The initial planning for cruises on their power boat *Lucky Lady* is done by spreading the charts out at home. They plan two routes to their destination. The first is a fairly direct route to be followed if the weather is clear. The other is planned in case there is restricted visibility; they then want to have as

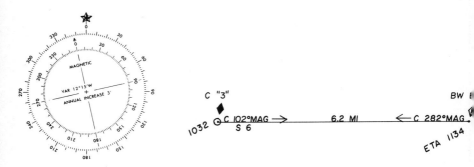

Fig. 7. Sample course line.

Course: 102° magnetic from 'C "3"' to 'BW BELL.'
Reciprocal course: 282° magnetic from 'BW BELL' to 'C "3"'.
Speed: 6 knots.
Mileage: 6.2 nautical miles.
Time that 'C "3"' is passed close aboard: 1032 (10:32 A.M.).
ETA (estimated time of arrival) at 'BW BELL': 1134 (11:34 A.M.).
This is determined by using the distance/speed/time formula for time and adding the answer to the time that the starting buoy is passed close aboard.

$$\frac{D \times 60}{S} = T \qquad \frac{6.2 \times 60}{6} = 62 \text{ minutes}$$

$$\begin{array}{r} 10^{\text{h}}32^{\text{m}} \\ +62^{\text{m}} \\ \hline 11^{\text{h}}34^{\text{m}} \text{ or } 1134 \end{array}$$

many opportunities as possible to check their course. A wide berth is given to aids marking navigational hazards, and buoys with sound signals are promoted to new positions of importance. In order to minimize error, all courses are figured by each of them and they recheck their charting if their figures do not agree.

Courses from buoy to buoy for the day's run are then listed consecutively. The information for each course includes:

Magnetic compass course to the next navigational aid.
Name and description of the navigational aid.
Sound and light characteristics of the aid.
Mileage and estimated running time between the aids.

Ship's Log Book

Strictly speaking, the ship's log book should be a formal chronicle of activities concerning the boat. Each page is dated and includes the entries for one day. Time is entered in twenty-four–hour time at the left of each entry. Entries include all three courses (true, magnetic, compass), weather (wind, sea conditions, barometer readings), and other relevant information.

Aboard cruising boats, information relative to the activities of the boat is viewed more broadly than it is aboard naval or commercial vessels. It can apply to anything from time and direction of a bearing to a list of guests who came aboard for cocktails that evening. It is possible over the years to build up in your log books a fund of information on different cruising areas, particularly when the information entered is chosen with this goal in mind. One problem in keeping a ship's log is to find the happy medium between having it as formalized as the USS *Missouri*'s log book or as chatty as a "Dear Diary" entry.

Every captain sets up his own rules for making entries in his ship's log. Our captains like their mates to attend to this and we pass along to you the types of ship's log entries which have proved meaningful to us.

Realizing a notebook from a five-and-dime is just not salty, we use a ship's log book purchased from a nautical supply store and write across the page, ignoring all the printed and labeled divisions. We reserve the left-hand page strictly for information pertaining to the boat and its movements, the right-hand page for chatter—idle or not, as the case may be.

The day of the week and the date are entered on the left side of the left-hand page. As frugal New Englanders, we often enter more than one date on a single page, but when we do this we always leave one blank line running across both pages before we start the entries for another date.

As we have pointed out, we draw and label our courses, bearings, and ranges in magnetic degrees directly on the chart. We must admit that the plotting figures rarely seem to make it to the ship's log book when cruising conditions are good, and whenever we do record degrees we record only the magnetic degrees. The number of entries in the ship's log book increases, however, during offshore races or when there is poor visibility due to fog, rain, or darkness. Then, entries are made from the DR (dead reckoning) track on the chart for every hour or course change. Whenever possible, bearings on navigational aids are recorded.

In fog, we record the number from the chart of each gong, whistle, or bell when we are sure of its identification—even though we do not see it and only hear the sound as we leave it to port or starboard.

On a clear day, entries on the left-hand page of the ship's log book might read:

1971
June 3, Wed.

0730	left Great Harbor. Mag. course 165°. Wind southerly 12–15. Seas slight.
0825	BELL "16" abeam ¼ mi. to stbd.
1110	Smith Point light and BELL "4" lined up. Bell about 1 mi. to stbd.
1350	wind gusting to about 20. Changed to #2 genoa. ETA Rocky Neck Harbor 1830.
1631	range on Gray Rock bell and radio tower at Pleasantville.
1802	entered Rocky Neck Harbor. NUN "6" close aboard. Turned on power.
1822	tied up at Hall's Marina

Entries for the page on the right side of the ship's log include all engine work, identification of any pictures taken, persons aboard, persons we have met and the name of their boat, notations like "shower is dirty" or "good washeteria at the top of the hill," as well as experiences and stories at sea or ashore.

One afternoon on the intracoastal waterway some distance north of Wrightsville, North Carolina, this stark statement was entered on the left-hand page of the Townsends' ship's log book: "1315–1325 mortar practice just behind us—shooting across waterway, but impact 1½ mi away E."

On the opposite page, however, is this story. "In the middle of the mortar practice, the *Fram*, Newport Beach, passed us. *Fram*'s skipper waved a white handkerchief to signal for a truce. I asked Sam to read the little sign at the edge of the waterway. He read 'Danger Area.'"

A later entry adds, "Sam confessed, the sign really said 'Impact Area.'"

Chart Table

The ideal situation is to have a chart table reserved solely for the navigator and his equipment, but on most family cruising boats the navigator has to make do by commandeering either the top of the ice chest or the cabin table. Nevertheless, there are three main requirements a navigator must consider before deciding on a place to ply his trade. He must be near equipment like the depth sounder and the RDF (radio direction finder), be able to communicate with the man at the helm, and have some method of keeping the drawing equipment in one place when charting in heavy weather.

Additional Plotting Tools

Parallel rulers and dividers are uncomplicated to use and therefore are good tools for beginning navigators. However, as you become more familiar with plotting courses and other techniques, we suggest you consider the possibility of using other plotting instruments as well. There are many of these on the market and each yachtsman has his favorites. We mention only a few here but we also suggest that you look over the different types in your local nautical supply store to find those best suited to your needs.

One of the easiest and quickest plotting instruments to use is the **rolling type of protractor.** The probability of making an error with this "one-handed" instrument is very small because of the unlikelihood of slippage. However, we find it is difficult to use this instrument if the charts have been folded because the rollers are likely to bump out of position as they are rolled over the fold.

This protractor consists of a wide, flat, clear-plastic ruler. One side of the ruler is inserted into a metal bar which is equipped with rollers at each end; the bar is removeable. Two circular scales are inscribed in the plastic ruler, one to be used with a parallel of latitude and the other to be used with a meridian of longitude. The circular scales are used to determine course or bearing degrees, and the long straightedge can be used to draw lines on a chart as well as to measure distances.

To use this type of plotter, line up the long straightedge on a course line (or between two points on a chart) and roll it across the chart until the positioning ' + ' in the center of the appropriate circular scale is placed on the nearest parallel of latitude or meridian of longitude on the chart. The *true* course degrees can be read from the degree angle of the circular scale. The "True Virgins Conversion Steps," described on page 44, can then be followed in order to determine a steering course.

We prefer to use magnetic degrees for our courses and bearings and we usually find that it is possible to line up the plotter on a course line (or between two points on the chart) in such a way that it can be rolled to the nearest compass rose. When the long straightedge is rolled to the ' + ' in the center of the compass rose, magnetic degrees can be determined from the inner circle of figures, which are identified by the word 'MAGNETIC'.

Although this type of plotter has a mileage scale on it for measuring distance, it is more accurate to determine mileage measurement from the latitude scales at the sides of a chart.

These roller plotters can usually be purchased from a nautical supply store for about $5.00. We are most familiar with the *C-Thru Paraglide protractor-plotter* (C-Thru Ruler Company, 6 Britton Drive, Bloomfield, Connecticut 06002) and the *Paraline plotter* (Weems & Plath, Inc., 48 Maryland Avenue, Annapolis, Maryland 21400).

The *Hurst plotter* (Brookes & Gatehouse, Inc., 154 Boston Post Road, Mamaroneck, New York 10543) is the only rotatable arm plotter that we have seen which makes it possible to determine courses easily in magnetic degrees. This plotter, which is imported from England, is rather expensive compared to the other tools we discuss.

The Hurst plotter is quick to use, avoids the possibility of error due to slippage, and eliminates the necessity of converting bearings and courses from true to magnetic degrees. It may be used to draw courses and bearings.

The Hurst plotter is comprised of a square of rigid clear plastic on which a grid is engraved. A circular 360° compass rose is inscribed on a clear plastic disc which is mounted on the gridded square by means of a locking device. A rotatable plotting arm is mounted between the grid and the rose, and can be rotated freely even when the disc is locked in position.

The locking device is released so that the rose on the plotter can be set to the variation figure given in the center of the nearest compass rose on the chart. Make sure that the variation direction on the plotter rose is on the same side of true north as the variation direction on the chart's compass rose, and that the direction of north is in agreement with the direction of north on the chart. The plotter is then placed on the chart so that the grid lines up with the latitude and longitude lines on the chart.

When plotting a course between two buoys, the ' + ' in the center of the plotter is placed on the first navigational aid while the plotting arm is swung so that it bisects the location dot of the second buoy. The magnetic course to that buoy can then be read from the rose on the plotter.

Parallel-lined plastic sheets are flexible rectangular sheets of clear plastic that have parallel lines inscribed in them. They are available at most nautical supply stores and offer an easy way to find the direction of a course drawn on a chart as well as a quick way to check the accuracy of course degrees which have been determined with another instrument.

The plastic sheet is laid on the chart so that one of the printed lines is parallel to a course line drawn on the chart while another line on the sheet intersects the center of the ' + ' in the middle of the compass rose.

The edge of these thin sheets of plastic cannot be used to draw a line. However, they can be rolled to be stowed, do not break when dropped, and are usually satisfactory to use on charts in an open cockpit. There is a mileage scale on one edge. We have used two makes of these flexible sheets, the *Courser* (Havilah S. Hawkins, Sedgwick, Maine 04676) and the *Chartmate* (West Products Corporation, P.O. Box 707, Newark, New Jersey 07100).

Binoculars

It is imperative to have a good pair of binoculars aboard to locate navigational aids, landmarks, and anything else you might have in mind. (We are enormously curious about the make, class, name, and home port of other boats. Often when unobtrusively using our binoculars to satisfy this urge, we find ourselves eyeball to eyeball with the working end of the binoculars on the other boat.)

A satisfactory all-around size for binoculars is 7 × 50. It is best to get those with individually adjustable eyepieces; they are usually sealed to protect the mechanism from corrosion in a salt water environment. When binoculars are used by several persons, it is more convenient to use those with a single adjustment for both eyepieces, but there is the possibility that the internal lens elements of this type of binoculars may become clouded.

Whenever we hand binoculars to guests, we drop the strap over their heads as a subtle indication of our unwritten rule that whenever binoculars are used they are to be attached to the person using them. We are sure this rule has many times saved the binoculars from a watery grave.

It is easy to steady the binoculars if you brace your hands by placing your thumb nails against the upper edge of your cheek bones. This method also makes it unnecessary to remove your sunglasses.

Without binoculars, it is possible to enhance your vision on the water by framing your eyes with your hands to cut down the glare. Overlap your fingers at your eyebrows and your thumbs at the bridge of your nose. Sweep the horizon as you would with binoculars and you will discover you can spot buoys and other navigational aids at a surprising distance with the naked eye.

6

Speed and Distance Indicators

THE NAVIGATOR'S JOB is simplified when both speed and distance indicators are part of the equipment aboard a boat. However, even one of these is very helpful, and it is possible to manage without either one if the state of your bank account makes this necessary. Even if you possess the most sophisticated equipment on the market, it also makes sense to learn back-up methods for estimating speed and distance aboard your boat.

Electrical Speed and Distance Indicators

Most marine speed indicators have a small propeller or paddle wheel which is installed to protrude from the underside of the hull. The rate of speed of the spinning of the rotor increases and decreases as the boat goes faster and slower. This *rate* of spin is recorded electrically and is usually demonstrated in knots by a needle on a speed gauge. If the instrument also has a distance indicator, the *number* of revolutions of the small rotor are recorded electrically, and nautical mileage is indicated on a digital distance gauge which is similar to a mileage meter in an automobile. Sometimes boats, like cars, have a trip indicator which may be set back to zero at the beginning of each course.

While speedometers and mileage meters on automobiles are expected to work merrily away year after year recording speed and mileage, it is quite a different story in a boat. Aside from the mechanical breakdowns of the instruments themselves, and these are legion, the speed sensor on the underside of the boat frequently becomes entangled with seaweed, or it can bend or even be broken off if it comes in contact with a submerged object. Any of these problems will cause inaccuracy in the speed registered on the gauge. As most distance indicators are connected to speed gauges, their accuracy is reliable only if the speed gauges are in good working order. Many speed gauges can be repaired from within the boat.

When the sensor mechanism is removed to check for damage or seaweed, the fountain of water which shoots into the interior of the boat, to say nothing of the repairer's face, before a hull plug can be inserted in its place, can be a very damp and exciting experience. The alternatives seem to be to swim underwater yourself, to hire a passing young man in a wet suit to inspect the damage, or to do without a speedometer until you get to a boat yard. So not only is it a good thing to have a back-up for an electric speed indicator, but it is also prudent to carry spare external replacement parts for the sensor should it become damaged or broken.

Taffrail Log

The taffrail log measures the distance a boat travels by means of a water-driven propeller called a **rotator**, which is towed astern at the end of a long line. It is attached to the upper part of the stern, or taffrail, of a boat.

The rotator spins as it is being towed behind a boat; the number of spins are counted mechanically and converted to nautical miles, which are registered on a recording instrument.

In one form or another, this way of measuring distance has been used on boats for a long time. The taffrail log is also referred to as a patent log, or Walker log, after the man who made improvements in it over a hundred years ago.

With some taffrail logs, you can also determine the speed the boat is moving through the water by noting the seconds it takes a contrasting color to rotate a specific number of times on the recording dial. The number of seconds is then compared to a speed chart supplied by the manufacturer for this purpose.

When you want to haul the taffrail log in to store it, the temptation is to pull it in hand over hand. But even if you carry out this operation smartly, the line is likely to twist and loop and end up in a big snarl. The proper way to bring in the rotator is to disconnect the line from the recording instrument first. Hold the line in one hand and drop the disconnected end overboard. Let the line slip through your hand so that it streams out astern as you pull in the rotator. Once the rotator is aboard, haul in the trailing line, coiling it neatly and compactly next to the rotator. Allow the coiled line to dry before stowing. All the twists in the line caused by the rotator have been removed by allowing the line to stream out astern.

The taffrail log should not be streamed astern until the boat is underway; otherwise it may become fouled in the propeller or sink to the bottom and catch on a rock. Also remember to bring in the taffrail log before entering a harbor or crowded area.

Occasionally imprudent fish have been known to let their appetites get the better of them and have swallowed the rotator. If the rotator is painted a dull black it may not end up as dinner, but it is a good precaution to have a spare rotator and line unit on hand.

For sailboats with stern pulpits, it may be more convenient

to purchase the sling type of taffrail log so that the recording instrument can be tied to the lifeline or stern pulpit instead of being permanently fastened to the taffrail.

Small-Boat Speed Indicators

There are many types of inexpensive speed indicators on the market which are suitable for small cruising boats.

In one type of speed indicator, the amount of resistance to the water offered by a line towed astern is measured by the pull exerted on a spring-loaded lever. As this pull increases or decreases, a needle moves around a printed dial to indicate the speed of the boat in knots.

Another type of speed indicator consists of a clear plastic tube which is held in the hand. A small ball is encased in the tube, which has a scale in knots printed on the outside. The end of the tube that has a hole in it is held overboard with the hole facing forward so that the water will force the ball up the tube. The position of the ball on the scale indicates the speed of the boat. The scale on a speed indicator for a sailboat should read from 0 to 10 or 12 knots, while the scale for one used aboard a power boat should have a much greater range.

Feet-per-Second Table for Determining Speed

If there is neither a speed nor a distance indicator aboard, there is a method which can be used to determine speed when the boat speed is not more than 6 or 7 knots.

Someone with a stop watch or a watch with a second hand is stationed on the bow of the boat. A small wad of paper or a match cover is thrown into the water from the bow as far forward as possible. Timing is started the moment the bow is even with the paper. When the paper reaches the transom, another crew member calls "Mark!" and the elapsed time is noted by the timekeeper.

To avoid littering, the time can be taken with a permanent object, such as a stake, a buoy, or a lobster pot, or even by throwing overboard a potato chip which the fish or seagulls will eat.

The number of elapsed seconds is used in the following formulas, which also use the overall length of the boat and the fixed number 1.69 (the number of feet traveled per second at a speed of one knot; it is arrived at by converting 6,076 feet per hour, which is equal to one knot, into feet per second).

$$\frac{\text{length of boat in feet}}{\text{seconds}} = \text{boat speed in feet per second}$$

$$\frac{\text{boat speed in feet per second}}{1.69} = \text{boat speed in knots}$$

For example, assume the boat length is 30 feet and the elapsed time is 5 seconds.

$$\frac{30 \text{ feet}}{5 \text{ seconds}} = 6 \text{ feet per second}$$

$$\frac{6 \text{ feet/second}}{1.69} = \underline{3.55 \text{ knots}} = \text{speed through the water}$$

As there is always the possibility a speed indicator will fail, this is a good back-up method to find speed. Since you know the overall length of your boat, you can make a speed table for several different elapsed periods of seconds while sitting by the fire at home on a rainy winter evening. Then, during the boating season, you can estimate your speed merely by dropping the paper overboard, timing your passage by it, and consulting your table.

Determining Speed or Distance with One Indicator Aboard

Aboard cruising boats equipped with only one indicator, speed or distance for more or less than one hour can be determined by using the distance/speed/time formula as mentioned in the previous chapter. When a boat has only a speed indicator aboard, distance can be determined by using the formula variation

$$D = \frac{S \times T}{60}$$

If there is only a distance indicator, speed can be determined by changing the formula to

$$S = \frac{60 \times D}{T}$$

Speed Relationship to rpm

Some skippers of boats under power determine boat speed through the water by readings on an instrument, such as a **tachometer,** which records the number of revolutions per minute (rpm) made by the engine. They make a table to determine the boat speed from various rpm readings. Yours can be made as follows:

For each engine speed likely to be used, make two runs, one in each direction of a course which can be measured on a chart, such as between two buoys. The runs should start far enough away from the first buoy so that the boat is moving at a constant speed through the water before it begins the measured run. Each run is timed and the total is averaged. The boat speed can then be determined for the different revolutions per minute recorded in the table by using the speed/time/distance formula.

Assume the distance between two charted buoys is 1.5 miles. Runs made in each direction average 7 minutes for the 1.5 miles. We use the formula

$$\frac{D \times 60}{T} = S$$

$\dfrac{1.5 \times 60}{7} = \underline{12.9 \text{ knots}}$, which corresponds to the noted rpm

Ideally, the runs used for setting up the table should be made under conditions of still water, light air, and slack current. Later, additional runs can be made under various conditions of sea and wind to compare their effect on the boat speed at the rpm readings recorded in the table.

At the time of the runs, the skipper must take into consideration the condition of the bottom of the boat and the propeller. The amount of water, gas, stores, and equipment as well as the number of persons aboard should be recorded. As the speed/rpm relationship in the table will be affected if there are any major changes in these variables, the skipper may wish to recheck the table from time to time to determine what effect these changes may have on the boat speed at a particular rpm reading.

Averaging Speed on Sailboats

When a boat is under sail, an estimate of the average knots registered on the speed gauge during each hour is used as an estimate of the distance, or mileage, traveled along a course in that hour. To determine the estimated distance traveled in less than an hour, use an average of the speed in that time in the formula

$$D = \frac{S \times T}{60}$$

7

Ranges

Two navigational aid structures are called a **range** when they are intended to be visually aligned. When a range is marked on a chart, it is intended to be a guide for the helmsman to stay within the limits of a channel. The symbols for the navigational aids of a range on the chart are connected by a dashed line which sometimes extends beyond one of them before it becomes the solid line intended as the course line. Often the word 'range' is included in the description on the chart.

In a booklet called *Marine Aids to Navigation*, the U.S. Coast Guard succinctly describes ranges and their inherent risks as follows:

> Ranges are two structures which, when appearing to be in line (i.e. one over the other) indicate to the mariner that he is on a safe course. They can be either lighted or not.
>
> By steering a course which keeps these structures in line the mariner will remain within the confines of the channel. Remember—ranges cannot be used for the entire time you can see them. Quite a few of them are on shore, and that's where you'll be if you don't consult your chart where to change course.

A navigator can use a range to estimate his progress along a course line. To do this he can use a charted range, but often he takes advantage of the positions of navigational aids and charted landmarks to set up his own ranges. He notes the time when two aids become visually aligned and draws a line on the chart through the range to the course line. The time the range is sighted is marked above this line and the word 'RANGE' is marked below this line. (See Fig. 8.)

As the boat is located somewhere along the line drawn from the range, this line is referred to as a single **line of position** (LOP). If you have confidence in your ability to estimate the distance from the nearest navigational aid in the range, you will have a rough idea of your location on this single line of position.

Estimating Distances from Navigational Aids

If you wish to enter in the ship's log book the time the range was aligned and the identification of the navigational aids used, be sure to include the estimate of your distance from the nearest aid, as "1253—NUN "2" in line with lookout tower on Eagle's Neck. NUN "2", $\frac{1}{4}$ mile to starboard."

You can train yourself in estimating distance by frequent testing. The Ericson family play a distance estimating game during long automobile trips. The driver chooses a distant structure and asks everyone to guess how far it is from a nearby point. He then checks the distance traveled on the odometer (mileage meter) and the closest guess wins.

The game is carried over to the boat with estimates of distances which can be checked, such as the distance to a buoy ahead on the course at a time of slack current. Checking the accuracy of the estimates can be done with a distance indicator or taffrail log. For boats equipped with only a speedometer, the accuracy can be checked by taking the time

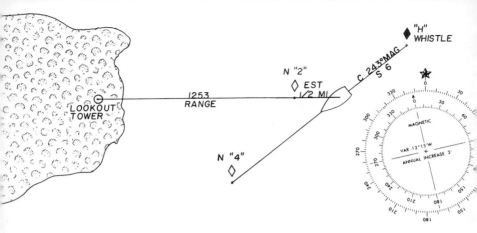

Fig. 8. Single line of position from a range.

Time that navigational aids are in line: 1253 (12:53 P.M.).
  (Boat is located somewhere along this line.)
Estimated distance from nearest aid, 'N "2" ': ½ mile.
    There is more opportunity to set up your own range with a buoy and a fixed object, as illustrated, but two fixed structures offer a more dependable range.

the estimates are made, maintaining a constant speed to the buoy, and using the formula

$$D = \frac{S \times T}{60}$$

It is amazing how much more accurate everyone becomes with practice in estimating distances on the water.

8

Bearings

A NAVIGATOR, particularly in coastal waters, makes frequent checks on the position of his boat. One way he accomplishes this is by taking bearings. In navigation, a bearing is the direction from a boat to a navigational aid or other charted reference point. When a bearing is drawn as a line on a chart, it is called a **single line of position** (LOP) because the boat is located somewhere along this line. In order to pinpoint the position of the boat on this line, it is necessary to take one or more bearings on other navigational aids that will cross each other when drawn on a chart. The point at which these bearing lines, or lines of position, intersect is a relatively accurate location of your boat, called a **fix** (see chapter 10).

Visual bearings are taken by sighting toward a navigational aid across a ship's compass, a handbearing compass, or a pelorus. Bearings taken with electronic instruments may be taken on points of reference which are not visible.

To Take a Bearing with a Ship's Compass

Line up a navigational aid with the center of the ship's compass and read the degrees of an imaginary line projected from the center of the compass to the aid. This will give you the compass bearing of the aid from the boat. If your compass has been compensated, this is also the magnetic bearing.

If your compass has not been compensated, note the compass reading for the *ship's heading* and apply the correction from your compass deviation table for this heading to the bearing. Work *up* the "True Virgins Conversion Steps" from compass to magnetic (or true).

As an example, assume a boat is heading 062°C (compass reading) when the navigator sights a standpipe across the ship's compass and it bears 107°C. The ship's compass deviation table gives a 5°W deviation for the compass reading of the ship's heading 062°C, and the course drawn on the chart is labeled 'C 057°MAG'.

We do not recommend labeling courses with magnetic degrees when there is deviation in the ship's compass, but if we did, we would also include the compass degrees in parentheses after the magnetic degrees, as '(062°C)'.

To avoid an error when writing down the letters to determine the magnetic degrees of a bearing, we repeat the memory aid "*T*rue *V*irgins *M*ake *D*ull *C*ompanions" to remember the order of "magnetic," "deviation," and "compass." We also remember "from true add west" so that when we are working up the steps, 'W' (west) is subtracted.

	Ship's Heading	Bearing	
M	057°MAG	102°MAG	(answer)
D	5°W	5°W	(from ship's heading)
C	062°C	107°C	(sighting)

A common error is to apply the ship's compass deviation for the bearing degrees to the bearing instead of applying the deviation for the boat's heading at the time the bearing is taken. It must be reemphasized that the direction in degrees on the ship's compass for the heading of the boat is the figure which reacts to magnetic influences aboard.

If you wish the degrees for your ship's heading to be in true degrees as well, the variation figure of the nearest compass rose is similarly applied to the magnetic degrees of the ship's heading. The completed table in calculating a case of this sort follows.

	Ship's Heading	Bearing
T	045°	090°
V	12°W	12°W
M	057°MAG	102°MAG
D	5°W	5°W
C	062°C	107°C

In order to plot a bearing line on the chart, you must start at the navigational aid since you do not know exactly where your boat is located. To do this, use the reciprocal (opposite direction) of the bearing by adding or subtracting 180°. In practice, however, if the parallel rulers are placed so that they intersect the compass rose across its diameter when they are positioned on the degrees of the bearing, they automatically fall on the reciprocal degrees on the opposite side of the compass rose. It is not necessary therefore to compute the reciprocal.

Once the parallel rulers are in the correct position on the compass rose, walk them across the chart to the aid and draw a line from the aid to your course line or beyond it. Write above this line the time the bearing was taken and indicate below the line the direction *from* the boat in magnetic degrees followed by the abbreviation 'MAG'. (See Fig. 9.)

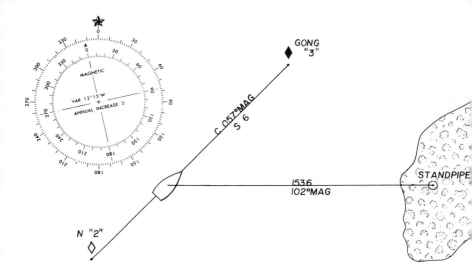

Fig. 9. One bearing—single line of position.

Course: 057° magnetic from 'N "2" ' to 'GONG "3" '.
Speed: 6 knots.
Bearing of standpipe from boat: 102° magnetic.
Time of sighting: 1536 (3:36 P.M.).
    (Boat is located somewhere along this line.)
        When there is deviation in the compass used for a bearing, use its
        deviation table and apply the deviation for the ship's heading to
        the compass bearing degrees in order to obtain the magnetic bear-
        ing degrees. Assume 5°W deviation at 062° compass.
                Ship's heading (from deviation table):
                        M   057°
                        D   5°W
                        C   062°
                For bearing, use deviation from above:
                        M   102°
                        D   5°W
                        C   107°

To Take a Bearing with a Handbearing Compass

A handbearing compass is a portable compass, and visual
bearings on navigational aids are taken by sighting across it.

The procedures are the same as taking a bearing with the ship's compass.

Before relying on bearings taken with a handbearing compass, the accuracy of the instrument when held in the position where it will be used should be checked by comparing it with the compensated ship's compass. If the readings are different, any bearings taken with a handbearing compass should be corrected. For example, if the ship's compass reading is 090° for the boat's heading and the reading on the handbearing compass for the same direction is 095°, subtract 5° from the bearing figure. If the reading is less on the handbearing compass, the difference is added.

Racing sailors use a handbearing compass to take comparative bearings on their competitors. By writing down the degrees of a bearing taken on the mast or bow of another boat and comparing them to the degrees of a bearing taken somewhat later on the same boat, it is possible to estimate which boat has gained during that period. If the angle between you and your opponent increases, you are gaining, and vice versa. When the boat in question is far away, it will gain or lose more for a given number of degrees than if it is nearby.

To Take a Bearing with a Pelorus

A pelorus is an instrument that has a circular disc called an azimuth card on which the degrees of a compass card are duplicated. In addition, there is a sighting device which is rotated over the azimuth card so that it can be lined up with a visible navigational aid. A pelorus is placed on a boat with 000° pointing forward and the 000°–180° axis parallel to the center line of the boat. The degrees of the direction of the navigational aid, as indicated by the position of the sighting device, are read from the pelorus. At the same time the navigator calls "Mark!" to the helmsman and notes the compass reading at that moment.

Any bearing taken with a pelorus or like nonmagnetic instrument is called a **relative bearing,** since the reading is obtained from a nonmagnetic compass card which has the reference degrees in a fixed position relative to the center line of the boat.

When relative bearing degrees are added to the ship's heading in compass degrees, the bearing is in compass degrees.

When the relative bearing degrees are added to the ship's heading in magnetic degrees, the bearing is in magnetic degrees which we use to plot bearings.

When the relative bearing degrees are added to the ship's heading in true degrees, the bearing is in true degrees.

Although we are guilty of using a very unsophisticated version of a pelorus to take relative bearings on navigational aids, the steps are the same as those used with a more conventional instrument. With our method, a circular protractor, which is usually available in a store that sells drawing instruments, doubles as the 360° azimuth card of a pelorus. (Our circular protractor is a clear plastic disc of about 4 inches in diameter with a positioning mark, or ' + ', in the center.) The stem of a short, sharp pencil is used as the sighting device. The pencil is grasped between the ends of two fingers which are then rested on the protractor on either side of the center positioning ' + '. The pencil point is just inside the degree markings. When the pencil is rotated, it serves as a sighting arm.

We take a relative bearing on a navigational aid by placing the circular protractor on the deckhouse or other flat surface where the view to the navigational aid is unobstructed. The protractor is positioned so that 000° is pointing forward and the 000°–180° axis parallel to the center line of the boat. As soon as the pencil-sighting arm is pointing at the navigational aid, the word "Mark!" is called to the helmsman, who calls back the compass degrees of the ship's heading. This compass heading is written down and added to the relative bearing reading from the circular protractor, as indicated by the point of the pencil-sighting arm for a compass bearing.

If the compass has been compensated, the compass degrees of the ship's heading will be the same as the magnetic degrees of the ship's heading at the time the bearing was taken. As you know, however, if the compass has not been compensated, the compass degrees of the heading as given by the helmsman will have to be converted to a magnetic heading by applying the proper deviation from the ship's compass deviation table before you can find the magnetic degrees of the bearing.

When the addition of the magnetic degrees of the heading and the relative bearing degrees from the pelorus total more than 360°, subtract 360° from that total. You now have the magnetic bearing from the boat to the navigational aid.

To illustrate: assume that the position of the pencil point over the circular protractor indicates the relative bearing of '204°' and that at this moment you call "Mark!" to the skipper, who tells you his compass heading is 285°C. Since the ship's compass is not compensated, you check the compass deviation table and determine that the deviation for a ship's heading of 285° is 3°W. According to your wrist watch, you took the bearing at 3:04 P.M., or 1504.

You work out the problem of converting the relative bearing to a magnetic bearing by using the "True Virgins Conversion Steps" as shown on page 92.

To plot the bearing on the chart, you place the parallel rulers across the magnetic rose at '126°MAG' and they automatically fall on the reciprocal '306°MAG'. You carefully walk the parallel rulers to the navigational aid and draw the bearing line from the aid to the course line. The bearing line is labeled with '1504' above the line for the time the bearing was taken, and with the bearing figure '126°MAG' (the magnetic degrees of the bearing you took) below the line.

Ship's
Heading (work up the steps)

M	282°	magnetic heading
D	3°W	deviation for 285°C
C	285°	compass heading

$$282°\text{MAG} \quad (\text{magnetic heading})$$
$$\underline{+204°} \qquad (\text{relative bearing from pelorus})$$
$$486° \qquad (\text{total more than } 360°)$$
$$\underline{-360°}$$
$$\underline{\underline{126°\text{MAG}}} \quad (\text{answer}): \text{ magnetic degrees of bearing on navigational aid from boat}$$

Navigational Aids Abeam

One of the easiest ways to take a single line of position is to note the time a navigational aid or charted landmark is **abeam** of the boat. A structure or aid is abeam when an imaginary line from the boat to it is at right angles to the center line of the boat. When taking this type of bearing it is essential that the boat is heading on the charted course at the time the sighting is recorded.

One way to plot this single line of position is to place one of the ends of the parallel rulers on the course line, so that one of the straightedges intersects the location dot of the navigational aid, and draw a line from the aid to the course perpendicular to the course line. This single line of position is labeled above the line with the time the structure or aid was abeam and below the line with the word 'ABEAM'.

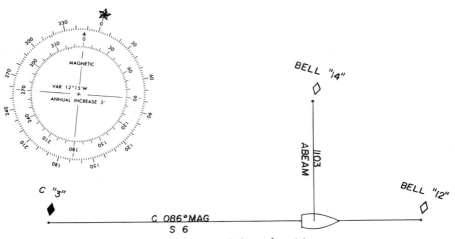

Fig. 10. Navigational aid abeam—single line of position.

Course: 086° magnetic from 'C "3" ' to 'BELL "12" '.
Speed: 6 knots.
Time that 'BELL "14" ' is sighted abeam: 1103 (11:03 A.M.).
(Boat is located somewhere along this line.)

Include your estimate of the distance from the navigational aid when recording this bearing in your ship's log book. This entry might read: "1103. BELL "14" buoy abeam, ½ mi to port."

Bow and Beam Bearing

It is possible to obtain a fairly accurate measurement of the distance a navigational aid is away from a boat when the aid is abeam. This method of measurement is called a **bow and beam bearing** and is based on the principle that when one angle of a right triangle is 45°, the two sides adjacent to the right angle are of equal length.

It is necessary to take two separate bearings on the same navigational aid. The first one is taken ahead of the boat to determine when a navigational aid bears 45° to the course line.

When the aid bears 45°, the mileage reading for the distance traveled along the course is noted. When the aid is 90° to the course line, or is abeam, a second distance reading is noted. The boat must be heading on the charted course during the entire time.

The distance the boat has traveled along the course between the two bearings is approximately equal to the distance between the boat and the navigational aid when it is abeam. If there is no distance indicator aboard, the elapsed time must be noted between the two bearings, a constant boat speed maintained, and the distance determined by the distance/speed/time formula

$$D = \frac{S \times T}{60}$$

Because of the variables in a bow and beam bearing, it is not considered accurate enough to be called a fix.

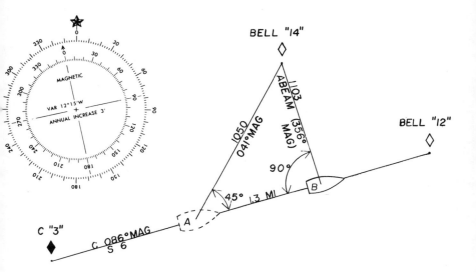

Fig. 11. Bow and beam bearing.

Course: 086° magnetic from 'C "3"' to 'BELL "12"'.

Speed: 6 knots.

Bow bearing: Boat at position 'A'; 'BELL "14"' bears 45° from course, 041° magnetic, at 1050 (10:50 A.M.).

Beam bearing: Boat at position 'B'; 'BELL "14"' bears 356° magnetic when it is abeam.

Time between bearings: 13 minutes (1103 minus 1050).

Distance traveled between bearings: 1.3 miles.

$$\frac{S \times T}{60} = D \qquad \frac{6 \times 13}{60} = 1.3 \text{ miles}$$

Distance from 'BELL "14"' at 1103: 1.3 miles.

   (Two adjacent sides of a right triangle are of equal length when one angle is 45°.)

      Note: Be sure your boat is heading on course at the time of the sightings.

9

Danger Bearings

WHEN THERE ARE SUBMERGED ROCKS OR REEFS in an area where you wish to make a course change, it is advisable to construct a danger bearing line. This is a bearing line which avoids the hidden obstructions and is drawn on your chart from your course line to a navigational aid or jut of land.

The degrees of this line are determined from the magnetic rose and, if your compass is not compensated, are converted to a compass bearing. The degrees are marked on the danger bearing line preceded by the letters 'DB' for danger bearing and followed by the letters 'CB' for compass bearing.

When a bearing on the navigational aid or jut of land is the same as the degrees of the compass bearing marked on the danger bearing line, it is safe to alter course.

Depending on the location of the hidden obstruction, the navigator may wish to note whether a greater or lesser amount of compass degrees in a bearing would give additional sea room. When this extra clearance requires a greater number of compass degrees than the danger bearing, 'OR MORE IS SAFE' is added to the label of the charted bearing line; when it requires a smaller number, 'OR LESS IS SAFE' is added.

> *Example 1.* Assume you are on course 012° magnetic and the DB (danger bearing) line to 'BELL "6" ' is 062° CB

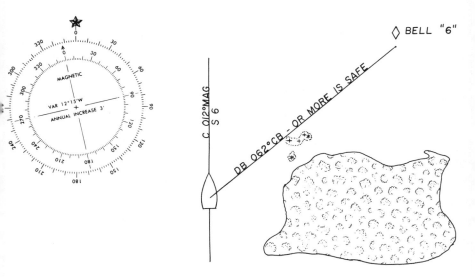

Fig. 12. Danger bearing (example 1).

Course: 012° magnetic.
Speed: 6 knots.
Danger bearing: At a compass bearing of 062° or more, it is safe to turn
toward 'BELL "6"'.
(Starred area denotes rocks.)

(compass bearing). As determined by the location of the
obstruction in the illustration, 'DB 062°CB—OR MORE
IS SAFE' is written on the danger bearing line. The label
on the danger bearing line tells you it is safe to alter
course to starboard when a bearing obtained from
sighting across the ship's compass to 'BELL "6"' is
062°CB or more, such as 067°CB.

Example 2. When you are on course 012°magnetic and
the danger bearing line to a jut of land is 332°CB, you
write '332°CB—OR LESS IS SAFE' on the danger
bearing line. This means it is safe to alter course to port
when a bearing taken on the jut of land is 332° or less,
such as 327°CB. (See Fig. 13.)

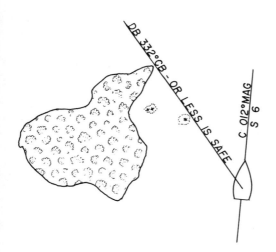

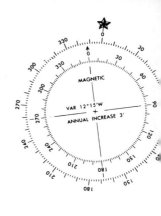

Fig. 13. Danger bearing (example 2).

Course: 012° magnetic.
Speed: 6 knots.
Danger bearing: At a compass bearing of 332° or less, it is safe to turn
toward jut of land.
(Starred area denotes rocks.)

10

Fix

IN NAVIGATING, a **fix** is assumed to be the actual position on a chart of a boat and it is established by crossed lines of position. The lines of position can be determined visually or electronically, but two or more visual bearings are considered to be the most reliable way to establish a fix.

A fix can be èstablished on a chart by two bearing lines which intersect at an angle of as near 90 degrees as possible, by three or more intersecting bearing lines, by a circle of distance (see chapter 12) intersected by a bearing line, or by two intersecting circles of distance. When three bearing lines drawn on a chart form a triangle where they come together instead of intersecting at one point, the location of the boat can be assumed to be in the center of this triangle.

A fix is labeled by making a small circle on the chart either at the intersection of two or more lines of position or around a dot marked in the center of a triangle formed by three bearing lines. This circle is identified with the time the fix is taken, such as '1156 FIX'.

When establishing a fix, two or more bearings should be taken as quickly as possible since it is convenient for the navigator, when plotting the bearing lines, to assume they are taken at the same time. This avoids the necessity of adjusting the position of any of the bearing lines to a common time.

If a fix does not coincide with the course line drawn on the chart, a new course line is started at the position of this fix and drawn to the same destination. The degrees of the new course are determined and recorded above the new course line with the boat speed written below the line.

For example, bearings on three navigational aids on charted structures are taken at 1030, while the boat is on a course of 102°MAG to C "3". These three aids bear 163°MAG, 228°MAG, and 268°MAG. By using the reciprocals of the bearings, lines are drawn on the chart from the navigational aids in the direction of the boat.

These bearing lines form a triangle at their junction, and the position of the boat is assumed to be at a dot marked in the center of this triangle. The dot is circled and labeled '1030 FIX'.

As this fix does not coincide with the course line drawn on the chart, a new course line is drawn from the fix to 'C "3"' , and the degrees of this course, or 'C 112°MAG', are written above the course line.

Sometimes the degrees of latitude and longitude of a fix are recorded in the ship's log book or written on the chart. However, in coastal waters, latitude and longitude are not usually figured for each fix since the navigator can determine this quickly if he wishes to report the boat's position in an emergency.

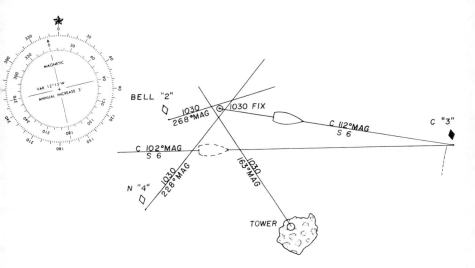

Fig. 14. Three-bearing fix.

Course: 102° magnetic (dashed outline of boat).
Speed: 6 knots.
Time that bearings are taken: 1030 (10:30 A.M.).
    (All three bearings are assumed to be taken at the same time.)
Bearings of navigational aids from boat:
       'TOWER'   163° magnetic
       'BELL "2"' 268° magnetic
       'N "4"'   228° magnetic
Fix: Circled dot in center of triangle formed by plotted bearings.
New course: 112° magnetic from fix to destination.

11

Running Fix

A **running fix** IS A FIX established by taking two bearings at different times, usually on the same navigational aid and from different locations along a course. A running fix can be used when there is only one navigational aid available on which to take bearings. It is not as reliable as a fix established by taking two or more bearings at the same time on different navigational aids, since its accuracy depends on a constant boat speed over the bottom between the two sightings. This is difficult to achieve.

If a running fix does not coincide with the course line drawn on the chart, a new course line is started at the position of this running fix and drawn to the same destination. The degrees of the new course are determined and recorded above the new course line.

Assume your boat is on course 102°MAG. There is no current, and the boat speed is 12 knots. On an otherwise empty horizon, you see one tall tower off the port bow and take a sight on it at 1250. The bearing on this tower is 075°MAG. With this information, the following steps demonstrate the method used to establish a running fix with a single navigational aid.

1. Place the parallel rulers across the compass rose at '075°MAG' to find the reciprocal and draw this single line

of position on the chart from the tower toward your course. Write '1250' over the bearing line and '075°MAG' under it.

2. Continue on course 102°MAG, maintaining a constant boat speed of 12 knots. At 1320, another bearing is taken on the same tower which is 003°MAG. Note the distance traveled from the first bearing. Using the reciprocal of the bearing, draw this single line of position on the chart from the tower toward your course. Write '1320' over the bearing line and '003°MAG' under it.

3. If you do not have a distance indicator aboard, figure the distance traveled between the times of the two sightings, 1250 to 1320, using the distance/speed/time formula in the following way:

$$13^{h}20^{m} \text{ (time of second bearing on the tower)}$$
$$\underline{- 12^{h}50^{m} \text{ (time of first bearing on the tower)}}$$
$$30^{m} \text{ (time elapsed between sightings)}$$

$$\frac{S \times T}{60} = D$$

$$\frac{12 \times 30}{60} = \underline{\underline{6 \text{ miles}}} \text{ traveled between sightings}$$

Mark this 6-mile distance along the course line from the first sighting. If the distance the boat has traveled over the bottom is accurate, this mark would be at the intersection of the '1320' bearing line and the course line. This probably will not happen since the boat speed is rarely the same as the speed over the ground because of the effect of current (see chapter 18), leeway (see chapter 19), and the inability of any helmsman to steer an absolutely steady course.

4. Place the parallel rulers on the '1250' bearing line and walk them across the chart until they meet the 6-mile

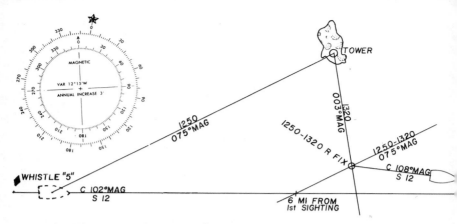

Fig. 15. Running fix on a single navigational aid.

Course: 102° magnetic.

Speed: 12 knots.

First bearing on 'TOWER': 075° magnetic, taken at 1250 (12:50 P.M.).

Second bearing on 'TOWER': 003° magnetic, at 1320 (1:20 P.M.).

Time between bearings: 30 minutes (1320 minus 1250).

Distance traveled between sightings: 6 miles.

$$\frac{S \times T = D}{60} \qquad \frac{12 \times 30}{60} = 6 \text{ miles}$$

Advanced bearing line: '1250–1320' (first bearing line advanced 6 miles).

Running fix: 'R FIX' (intersection of advanced and second bearing lines).

New course to destination: 108° magnetic (from 'R FIX').

mark made in step 3. Draw a line here which will intersect both the '1320' bearing line and the 6-mile mark on the course line. Write '1250–1320' above this **advanced bearing line** and '075°MAG' below the line.

5. Where line '1250–1320' intersects the '1320' bearing line, draw a small circle for the running fix and label it '1250–1320 R FIX'.

6. Because this running fix does not coincide with the course line, draw a new course line from the running fix to the same destination. Determine the degrees of this course line, in this case '108°MAG', and write them above the line with the boat speed below the line.

12

Circle of Distance

A **circle of distance** IS A CIRCLE drawn on a chart for a measured distance around a navigational aid. This is one more method by which the navigator can check the position of the boat.

When the height of a navigational aid is noted on a chart, a circle of distance can be used in the *daytime* to determine a single line of position, which is referred to in nautical lingo as an "LOP." If a bearing is also taken on this navigational aid and plotted on the chart as well, a fix is established where the bearing line intersects the circle of distance.

At *night,* a circle of distance can be plotted to determine the approximate time the light should become visible by using the mileage figure (geographical range) given on a chart for a lighted structure.

A circle of distance is drawn on a chart around a navigational aid by using a **drawing compass.** Some dividers can be converted to a drawing compass by exchanging one of the points for a pencil lead. The less sophisticated model, which is probably available in Junior's pencil box, has a pencil for one of its legs.

To Use in Daylight

Using a single structure, a circle of distance and a bearing can be plotted to establish a fix on a chart. The angle of the height of the structure above the horizon is measured by sighting from your boat with an instrument like a stadimeter or a sextant. With this measurement, the distance of the structure from your boat can be computed from a "Distance by Vertical Angle" table published by the U.S. Hydrographic Office. For accuracy in areas of a large tidal range, check the *Tide Tables* (see appendix I) because heights are given on charts in feet above mean high water. The mean high water figures for a few key places are given on some harbor and coast charts in a 'Tidal Information' table.

A ·drawing compass is placed on the latitude scale to measure off the computed distance. Holding the compass at this measurement, place the pointed leg on the location dot of the lighthouse and with the pencil leg draw a circle of distance around the structure. Write the distance with the abbreviation 'MI' on the outside of the circle of distance. The time the sighting was taken on the lighthouse is written inside the circle.

A bearing is also taken on the lighthouse at the time of the sighting. Using the reciprocal of the bearing (by adding or subtracting 180°), draw a bearing line from the structure to the course line; label it above the line with the same time used on the circle of distance and below the line with the magnetic degrees of the direction to the structure from the boat. The point where this bearing line intersects the circle of distance is a fix. It is marked with a small circle, the time sightings were taken, and the word 'FIX'.

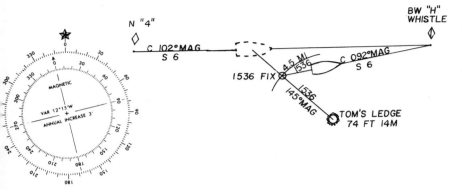

Fig. 16. Circle of distance—daylight.

Course: 102° magnetic from 'N "4" ' to 'BW "H" WHISTLE'.
Speed: 6 knots.
Distance from 'TOM'S LEDGE' at sighting: 4.5 miles (determined by a measuring instrument).
    Circle of distance is drawn.
Bearing of 'TOM'S LEDGE': 145° magnetic at 1536 (3:36 P.M.).
Fix: Intersection of circle of distance and bearing line.
New course to destination: 092° magnetic.

To Use at Night

A circle of distance from a lighthouse can be measured and drawn on the chart to determine the approximate time the light from this lighthouse should first become visible. The geographic range of a lighthouse is shown on the chart with the letter 'M' preceded by the number of nautical miles. The geographic range takes into consideration the curvature of the earth's surface and describes the distance a light can be seen in clear weather by an observer whose eye is 15 feet above the level of the water.

Since the geographic range does not take the candlepower of the light into consideration, a luminous range figure is given in the *Light List* (see appendix I), which may be different from the geographic range. The **luminous range** is the distance a light may be seen in clear weather and is given only for lights which can be seen for a distance of 5 miles or more. By using the "Luminous Visibility" diagram in the *Light List* it is possible to adjust the luminous range figure to show changes in the distance it can be seen according to the visibility in various weather conditions. A light cannot be seen beyond its geographic range for your height of eye even though the figure given for the luminous range may be greater.

When your eye level is higher or lower than 15 feet above sea level, you can use the "Distances of Visibility for Objects of Various Elevations Above Sea Level" table in the *Light List*. To use this table, estimate the height your eye is above the surface of the water and find the distance figure for this height in the table. Then read the height of the structure in question in the *Light List* or on the chart and find the distance figure in the table for this height. Add the two distance figures to find the geographic range of the light at your eye level.

In the following example of charting we will assume your eye level is 15 feet above the water and that the light from a lighthouse can be seen at the geographic range of 9 miles, which is given on the chart as '9M'.

Place your drawing compass on the latitude scale and measure off a distance of 9 miles. With the pointed end of the drawing compass on the dot in the center of the lighthouse symbol, draw a circle of distance 9 miles around the lighthouse. In clear weather, the light from the lighthouse should become visible at the point where this circle of distance intersects your course line.

The geographic range is marked on the outside of the circle as 'VIS 9 MI' for visibility 9 miles. The name of the lighthouse is written inside the circle.

Assume your boat speed is 6 knots, the time of your last known position was 2115 at BELL "2", and the distance from this buoy to the point where the circle of distance from Rocky Neck Lighthouse intersects your course line is 5 miles. First, determine how many minutes it will take your boat to travel

the 5 miles by using the following variation of the distance/
speed/time formula.

$$\frac{60 \times D}{S} = T$$

$$\frac{60 \times 5}{6} = \underline{\underline{50 \text{ minutes}}}$$

Add the 50 minutes to the time BELL "2" was passed close
aboard.

21^h15^m (time at BELL "2")

$+ \quad 50^m$

$\underline{22^h05^m}$ (answer): light should become visible at 2205
from a height of 15 feet

To determine the estimated direction from which the light
will first be visible to you, draw a dashed line from the point
where the circle of distance intersects the course line to the
lighthouse symbol. Draw a small circle around this intersection
and label it with the time the light should become visible.
Write the magnetic degrees of the bearing below the line
followed by the letters 'MAG'. Above the line, write the time
the light should become visible.

If you position yourself on your boat so your eye level is
approximately 15 feet above the water, to comply with the
geographic range of the lighthouse, the light should become
visible at 2205 in the direction of the compass bearing, or
033°MAG in this example.

Because it is difficult to establish the height of an eye above
the level of the water accurately and because the luminous
range of a light is affected by atmospheric conditions, the
intersection of the bearing line and the circle of distance of a
light is not considered a fix.

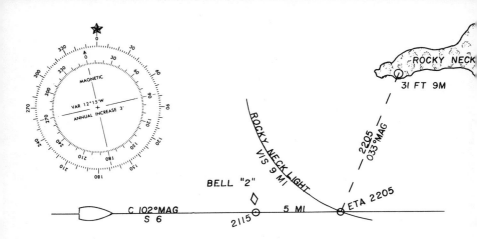

Fig. 17. Circle of distance—night.

Course: 102° magnetic.

Speed: 6 knots.

Time that 'BELL "2"' is passed abeam: 2115 (9:15 A.M.).

Distance at which light first becomes visible: 9 miles.

Circle of distance is drawn. (The geographic range of the visibility assumes a 15-foot height of the eye.)

Distance from 'BELL "2"' to intersection of circle of distance with course line: 5 miles.

Time that light should become visible: 2205 (10:05 P.M.).

$$\frac{60 \times D}{S} = T \qquad \frac{60 \times 5}{6} = 50 \text{ minutes}$$

$$\begin{array}{r} 2115 \\ +50 \\ \hline 2205 \end{array}$$

Bearing of light when it should become visible: 033° magnetic.

(In this case the intersection of the bearing line and the circle of distance is not reliable enough to be considered a fix.)

13

DR (Dead Reckoning) Track

WHEN NAVIGATING during times of poor visibility, such as in a fog or heavy rainstorm, or for several hours out of sight of land- or seamarks, it is essential to keep an hourly record on a chart of the boat's progress along a course. This is accomplished by **dead reckoning,** which is the method used to determine the probable position of a boat along a course, as estimated from the last fix or by passing a navigational aid close aboard. When dead reckoning positions are systematically recorded on a course line, this line is referred to as a **DR track.**

Keeping a DR track should be practiced many times in clear weather when you can check your accuracy visually. Then, when visibility lessens, you will have confidence in your ability to use this method of navigation. Ordinarily, of course, it is rarely used in buoy-to-buoy navigation when the distance between navigational aids is too short to warrant it and the visibility is good.

The DR position for every whole hour is usually recorded on the DR track. Each DR position is identified with a small circle labeled with the time of the reckoned position and the letters 'DR', such as '1800 DR'. Additional calculations of DR positions made at other times are labeled in the same way.

These calculations would be made also whenever the course is altered or the speed is changed.

The latitude and longitude of DR positions must be measured in order to enter them in the ship's log book. However, since hourly DR positions, fixes, or running fixes are plotted on the chart, we usually do not record them. Should an emergency arise we could very quickly compute the distance traveled from the last DR position plotted on the chart and then measure the latitude and longitude of our present DR position.

The distance traveled on the DR track from a fix or a previous DR position can be read from a distance indicator. It can also be calculated by using the distance/speed/time formula. When a boat is under sail, an estimate of the average speed is used in the formula.

Assume you are cruising offshore on course 102°MAG at a speed of 6 knots and there is no current. The visibility is fair, but you suspect before long a fog may close in on you. You pass C "3" close aboard at 0933 and record this time on the chart. This will be the beginning of your DR track.

Your DR position is plotted at the next whole hour, or 1000, by marking off on the DR track the distance the boat has traveled since C "3" was passed close aboard. If you do not have a distance indicator, you determine this distance by using the distance/speed/time formula in the following manner:

$$10^h00^m \text{ (next even hour)}$$
$$\underline{-09^h33^m \text{ (fix at C "3")}}$$
$$27^m \text{ (time from C "3")}$$

$$\frac{S \times T}{60} = D$$

$$\frac{6 \times 27}{60} = \underline{\underline{2.7 \text{ miles}}} \text{ from C "3" to 1000 DR position}$$

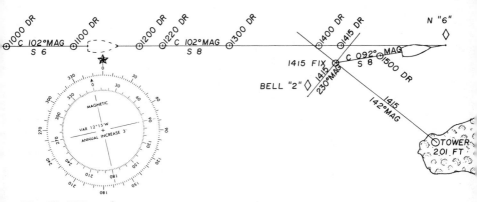

Fig. 18. DR track.

Course: 102° magnetic from 'C "3" ' to 'N "6" '.
Speed (original): 6 knots.
Time that 'C "3" ' is passed close aboard: 0933 (9:33 A.M.).
Time till next whole hour: 27 minutes (1000 minus 0933).
Distance covered at next whole hour: 2.7 miles.

$$\frac{S \times T = D}{60} \qquad \frac{6 \times 27}{60} = 2.7 \text{ miles}$$

(DR position recorded hourly between 'C "3" ' and 'N "6" '.)
Change of speed, recorded 1220 (12:20 P.M.): 8 knots.
Fix: Established at 1415 (2:15 P.M.) at intersections of bearings 142°
    magnetic and 230° magnetic.
New course to 'N "6" ': 092° magnetic.
    (New DR track started at fix.)

Measure 2.7 miles on the latitude scale and mark it on the
DR track. Draw a small circle around the measurement mark,
identifying it with '1000 DR'.

Either of the following methods can be used to measure
distance on the DR track. A drawing compass or dividers can
be used to measure this distance on the latitude scale and to
mark it off on the DR track. When dividers are used, the
distance can be marked by making a tiny hole with the point
of the dividers next to the DR track and by marking a pencil
stroke across the track at the hole.

The distance as measured from the latitude scale can also be
marked off on the edge of a piece of paper. The edge of the
paper then is laid along the DR track with the first mark of the

measurement placed at the last fix or DR position. Draw a short line perpendicular to the DR track at the place where the second mark falls.

The DR position is determined and marked on the chart in the same way every hour thereafter. Whenever it becomes possible to get a fix, this is recorded in the usual manner. If the fix does not coincide with the DR track, as occurs in the illustration of this problem, a new DR track is started at the position of this fix and drawn to the same destination. The degrees of the new course are determined, in this case '092°MAG', and recorded on the chart above the new DR track. The new boat speed of 8 knots, changed at '1220' as recorded on the DR track, is written below the line.

14

Plotting Tacks—Power and Sail

THUS FAR WE HAVE ASSUMED that the skipper of a boat is planning to adhere as closely as possible to the most direct course to his destination. There are times, however, when this is either unwise or impossible and he must resort to zigzag courses. This type of maneuver is referred to as **tacking** aboard boats under sail, and each course is called a **tack**.

Tacking Under Power

Although one might assume that the quickest way for a boat under power to travel between two points is along a straight line, it is not always true when the boat must be driven head-on into rough, cresting seas. When a boat shudders to a near stop with each wave, its overall progress is hampered and the severe pounding which occurs when it smashes directly into large waves can strain the hull. Under these conditions, a tacking maneuver can be adopted so that the boat is steered to cut through the waves at an angle, such as 45°, away from and back to the direct course. When this is done, the boat speed will usually increase enough to warrant traveling the extra distance, and the severe pounding should be alleviated. We refer to this as **tacking under power.**

When this condition prevails, it is worthwhile to try a 45° tack long enough to determine an average boat speed. Then you can plot your probable progress to a destination in order to decide whether it is faster and better to continue on the direct course or to adopt the tacking maneuver.

A straight line is drawn on your chart between two points, and as you remember, this is referred to as a **rhumb line.** For the purposes of this plotting, two hours is a convenient time period to use.

As an example, assume your boat speed is 3 knots when you are heading directly into the seas while following a direct rhumb line course to your destination. When you alter course 45° to cut through the waves obliquely, you find your average boat speed increases to 6 knots.

In Fig. 19, which compares the progress made when steering along the rhumb line for two hours with the progress made when steering two one-hour tacks, the departure in both cases is 'C "3" '; the rhumb line course is '000°MAG'; the first tack of '045°MAG' is away from the rhumb line; and the second tack of '315°MAG' is back to it.

1. The boat on the rhumb line, making 3 knots (nautical miles in one hour), would travel 6 miles in two hours. Measure this distance on the latitude scale and make a mark on the 'C 000°MAG' rhumb line 6 miles from the departure point, 'C "3" '.

2. Then, from 'C "3" ', draw a line, 'C 045°MAG', for the first tack. Since the boat speed when heading on a 45° angle to the oncoming seas is 6 knots, measure 6 miles on the latitude scale and mark off 6 miles on this tacking line for one hour of travel in this direction.

3. From this 6-mile mark on tacking line '045°MAG', draw tacking line 'C 315°MAG' back to the rhumb line, thereby plotting the second hour of tacking.

4. Determine the mileage which the boat would have progressed along the rhumb line by measuring from the beginning of the first tacking line at 'C "3" ' to the end of the second tacking line. In this example, the boat would be a distance of 8.5 miles along the rhumb line during a two-hour tacking maneuver.

According to this plot, therefore, tacking is the faster way to advance along the rhumb line. Ignoring leeway, at the end of two hours the boat would be 2.5 miles farther along the rhumb line, when tacking, than if it were steered directly along the rhumb line course.

When auxiliary sailboats and motor sailers are tacking under power, they will usually gain additional speed if sails are raised even if the sails do not draw a hundred percent effectively.

Tacking in a Sailboat

When the course to a destination is directly into the wind, it is necessary for a sailboat to sail zigzag courses. In addition to this being called "tacking," it is also referred to as **beating to windward, going to windward,** and **going upwind.** When the wind is blowing over the starboard side of the boat, the boat is on a **starboard tack;** when the boat is turned to bring the bow directly into the wind and then swung so that the wind blows over the other side, the maneuver is called **coming about;** and when the wind blows over the port side of the boat, the boat is on a **port tack.**

Not only is it considerably more difficult for the navigator to plot tacks for a sailboat than for a power boat, but because of the flukiness of the strength and direction of the wind, it is also difficult to be assured of the outcome of the plotting. However, it is important for the navigator on a sailboat to be able to make a plot, even if it has to be readjusted should there be a shift in the wind.

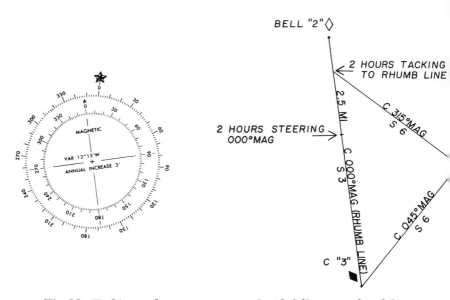

Fig. 19. Tacking under power compared with following a rhumb line.

Boat speed along rhumb line: 3.0 knots (6 miles in 2 hours).
Boat speed 45° from rhumb line: 6.0 knots (two 1-hour tacks).

Ignoring leeway, a boat is 2.5 miles farther along a rhumb line when it can make 6 knots tacking than it would be if it could only make 3 knots heading directly into head seas and strong winds.

When making a plot for a sailboat beating to windward, begin by drawing a straight line on a chart between two points. This rhumb line serves only as a reference line. In this case, the word "course" is reserved for the averaged compass direction of each tack away from and back to this rhumb line.

In order to plot the tacks, it is necessary to determine the **tacking angle** of your boat. The tacking angle is the difference in degrees between one tack and another. This can be done by beating to windward and taking a compass reading on one tack, coming about, and taking a compass reading on the other tack. When one compass reading is subtracted from the other, the result is the tacking angle of your boat.

When beating to windward, the heading is changed to follow the wind shifts; and since you do not steer a compass course, you may assume for plotting purposes your averaged heading or compass course is one half the tacking angle to an averaged wind direction.

As even a fairly steady wind will fluctuate a few degrees, the average wind direction should be determined by heading the boat directly into the wind several times, noting the compass degrees, and averaging these degrees. **Wind degrees** refer to the direction from which the wind is blowing, so that a wind blowing from the east is 090°.

Because it is not possible to correct for the angle of leeway, or sideway slippage, of the boat when sailing to windward, the track your boat will actually travel on the course over the ground (COG) is also drawn on the chart. When a modern sailboat is beating to windward under normal conditions, a leeway angle of 3° to 4° can be assumed. With strong winds, this leeway angle can increase to as much as 10° (see chapter 19).

Fig. 20 illustrates the practical application of the following steps. A rhumb line is drawn between 'N "8" ' and 'BELL "3" '. Since we are working in this problem with readings taken directly from the compass rather than magnetic degrees taken from a compass rose on a chart, as we have done in the majority of previous problems, we will use *compass degrees* in the plotting. (As you know, if your compass has been compensated these will also be magnetic degrees.)

Assume:

A rhumb line direction of '082°C' (compass)
A rhumb line distance of '13.2 MI' (miles)
A tacking angle of '90°'
A leeway angle of '4°'
An averaged wind direction of '072°C' (compass)
No current

1. Label the rhumb line '082°C' (compass degrees) and '13.2 MI'.

2. Determine the averaged windward compass course for the first tack by applying half the tacking angle, '45°', to the wind direction of '072°C', according to the desired direction of the first tack.

    072°C   (averaged wind direction)
    − 45°   (half the tacking angle)
    C 027°C = averaged compass course or heading for first tack

3. Determine the compass degrees for the COG (course made good over the ground) by applying the leeway angle of '4°' to the averaged compass course, 'C 027°C'.

    C 027°C   (averaged compass course)
    −   4°   (leeway angle)
    COG 023°C = averaged course over ground

4. Place the center of a circular protractor on the location dot of 'N "8" ', the starting buoy from which the rhumb line is drawn. Rotate this protractor until 082° falls on the '082°C' of the rhumb line. Keeping it in this position, make pencil marks at the edge of the protractor at:

072° for averaged wind direction.
027° for averaged compass course.
023° for averaged COG.

5. Draw a line from the 'N "8" ' location dot to the wind direction pencil mark and label it '072°C' above and 'WIND' below.
    6. Draw a dashed line from the 'N "8" ' location dot through the pencil mark for the averaged compass course and label it 'C 027°C'.
    7. Draw a line from the 'N "8" ' location dot through the pencil mark for the averaged COG and label it 'COG

023°C'. This will be the course your boat will make good on the first tack.

Although you determined a tacking angle of 90° was possible for your boat, the tacking angle made good is actually 98° because of the 4° leeway which is expected for each tack. To determine when to come about, it is necessary to plot the COG for the second tack *from* the destination buoy by using half this 98° tacking angle made good, or 49° to the wind. You will come about for the second tack at the point where this line intersects the COG of the first tack. The following steps explain how to plot the line for the second tack.

8. Place parallel rulers on the averaged wind direction line, and walk them to the location dot of the destination buoy, 'BELL "3" '. Draw a second averaged wind direction line to 'BELL "3" ', and label this '072°C' above and 'WIND' below.

9. Placing the center of the circular protractor on the 'BELL "3" ' location dot, rotate it until 000° is on this wind direction line. Make a pencil mark along the edge of the protractor at half the tacking angle made good, or 49°.

10. Draw a line from the pencil mark for half the tacking angle made good through the 'BELL "3" ' location dot and continue it to intersect the line of the first COG. Find the degrees of the new COG by applying the entire 98° tacking angle made good to the 'COG 023°C' on the first tack. Label this line 'COG 121°C'.

11. Place the center of the circular protractor at the intersection of the two COG lines, measure 4° for leeway, and draw a dashed line from the intersection to the rhumb line which has been extended beyond 'BELL "3" '. To find the compass degrees for this second compass course, apply 4° of leeway to the second tack COG. Label this line 'C 117°C'. The distances of both

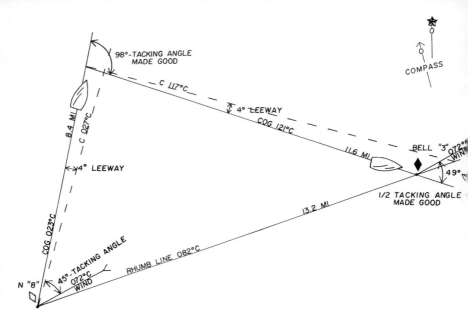

Fig. 20. Sailboat beating to windward (no current).

Rhumb line: 082° compass, 13.2 miles.
  (This is used as a reference line.)
Wind direction: 072° compass (averaged).
Tacking angle: 90°.
  (Compass readings taken aboard the sailboat between tacks.)
First tack (figured from 'N "8"'):
  Averaged heading expected: 027° compass (wind, 072°C, minus
    half of tacking angle, 45°).
  Leeway angle: 4° (assumed).
  COG: 023° compass ('C 027°C' minus '4° LEEWAY').
  Tacking angle made good: 98° (tacking angle of 90° plus 4° lee-
    way on each tack).
Second tack (figured from 'BELL "3"'):
  COG: 121° compass (half of tacking angle made good, 49°, plus
    wind, 072°C).
  Averaged heading expected: 117° compass (121° COG with 4°
    leeway applied).

COGs are measured from a latitude scale on the chart. In this
illustration, the distance made good for the first tack is 8.4
miles and for the second, 11.6 miles.

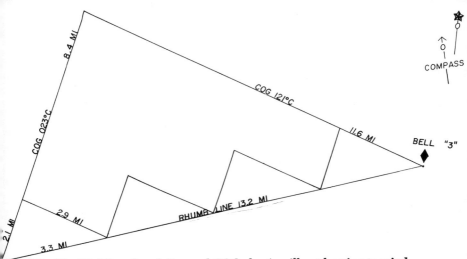

Fig. 21. Dividing rhumb line and COGs by 4, sailboat beating to windward (no current).

(Based on Fig. 20.)

A record is kept of the distance actually traveled by the boat on each tack, away from and back to the rhumb line. This distance can be measured either with a distance indicator or by using the distance/speed/time formula

$$D = \frac{S \times T}{60}$$

The figure used in the formula for the boat speed is the averaged speed for the length of the tack.

If the distance the boat travels away from the rhumb line seems particularly long, you may prefer instead to make several shorter tacks. This can be plotted by deciding on the number of additional tacks away from the rhumb line you wish to make. Divide this number into the mileage of the COGs which you determine when you plot two long tacks (one away from and one back to the rhumb line). For example, should you prefer to make four shorter tacks away from the rhumb line, instead of one long tack as plotted above, the tacks to 'BELL "3" ' would be plotted, according to the COGs in Fig. 20. (See Fig. 21.)

Whenever the helmsman notifies the navigator of any major sustained wind shift, the navigator must note the time, figure the distance along the leg when the shift occurred by using the formula

$$D = \frac{S \times T}{60}$$

and then replot the tacks using the new wind direction.

15

Depth Sounding

THERE ARE MANY TIMES when it is important to be able to determine the depth of the water under your boat, such as when entering a harbor, finding a spot to anchor for the night, or checking to determine the boat's probable location along a charted course.

Depth Sounders (Electronic Echo Sounders)

A **depth sounder** or **echo sounder** is an electronic device which almost instantaneously shows the depth of the water under the boat. A depth sounder includes a transducer, which is installed in the lower part of a hull as close as possible to the center line and transmits ultrasonic pulses into the water. These ultrasonic pulses bounce off the bottom, and the resulting echo is received by the transducer. The time the pulse takes to make the trip is measured and converted to a depth reading in feet or fathoms on the depth sounder indicator.

The indicator should be positioned where it can be seen by both the helmsman and the navigator, but it must be at least 2 feet away from the ship's compass or else it may attract the magnetic compass needle. The location of the indicator for the electronic depth sounder is an important consideration in the type of instrument you purchase. A flashing light indicator, which is divided like a clock face to read in either 60 feet or 60 fathoms, is easy to interpret from a distance, particularly if the face is never in bright sunlight. In some wheelhouses, or when the indicator is mounted on a hinged swing-away panel in the companionway, bright light may make it difficult to read. When this is the case, it might be preferable to have a meter-type readout—a pointer or needle indicates the depth on a dial in a manner similar to an automobile speedometer needle. Another type of indicator is the digital readout; in this case the feet or fathom digits can be read on the face of the instrument.

There are also instruments which record a tracing of the depths. Although this type of depth sounder is comparatively more expensive, it has the advantage of presenting an instant record of the changing depths of the course the boat has been traveling over the ground. This can then be compared with soundings marked on the chart. The recording type is also of value to fishermen because it records the presence and depths of schools of fish.

In order to compare the depth readings on the indicator dial with the mean low soundings printed on a chart, you may want the type of indicator dial which can be adjusted to show the depth of the water (from the bottom to the surface) no matter where the transducer is located in the hull. In this case, you will have to subtract the draft of your boat from the depth sounder reading to determine the depth of water beneath your keel.

The flashing light type of depth sounder and the recording type usually show the different characteristics of the bottom. For example, a thin line depicts a hard bottom; a wide band of blurred lines, a soft or muddy bottom.

Transducers on depth sounders have an average life of three to five years. When you notice that the sensitivity of your depth sounder is not what it used to be, a qualified technician should be called in to check this, and a new transducer should be installed if necessary.

A Series of Soundings

Where distinct depth changes are shown on the chart along your probable course, even the nonrecording type of depth sounder can be used to determine the probable location of your boat by systematically comparing its readings with the chart.

To do this, make up a **distance-depth** record of your boat's course over the ground. Take a series of readings from the depth sounder at equal time intervals while the boat is moving at a constant speed and on a specific course. Calculate the distance traveled through the water by using the distance/speed/time formula variation of

$$D = \frac{S \times T}{60}$$

For example, assume the boat has been moving at 6 knots (speed) and you have taken several depth sounding readings at 5-minute intervals (time).

$$\frac{S \times T}{60} = D; \text{ thus, } \frac{6 \times 5}{60} = 0.5 \text{ mile traveled during each 5-minute interval}$$

Use the latitude scale on the side of the chart and mark the edge of a sheet of tracing paper into 0.5-mile segments. Write down the appropriate depth readings for each 0.5-mile mark.

As chart soundings are for mean low water, the number of feet calculated from the *Tide Tables* (see appendix I) must be added to or subtracted from these soundings to find the depth of the water for a specific time and place.

Your distance-depth record can now be compared with the soundings printed on the chart. Line it up in the direction of your course and move it around on the chart in the area of the probable location of your boat until the depth notations on the distance-depth record approximate the depths given on the chart.

We accept a position arrived at by this method with some reservation. However, it is always reliable in a negative way, because if your distance-depth record is completely different from the depths shown on the chart, you know for sure where you are not.

Following a Fathom Line

Depth sounder readings can be used as a guide for steering along a fathom line. Check the chart along either side of the selected fathom line for sudden shoaling or rocks, because your course is likely to deviate slightly from this line. A single visual bearing can pinpoint your position on this fathom line.

Zigzagging in a Channel

In a poorly marked or unlighted dredged channel, some skippers suggest watching the depth sounder carefully and steering a zigzag course, slowly moving from one side of the channel to the other. The course is altered as the channel starts to shoal on each side. This suggestion is reasonable because, if you have not steered a zigzag course and run aground in the channel during fog or at night, you risk becoming confused and could turn the wrong way, driving your boat harder aground.

Lead Line

This sounding device has been used almost as long as there have been boats, but if you have an electronic depth sounder, the lead line is often relegated to the less important position of back-up.

The lead line is a length of line usually marked in fathoms (and sometimes half-fathoms) with a lead weight at one end. This weight has an indentation in the bottom which should be packed with a sticky substance such as waterproof grease. Theoretically, particles from the bottom will adhere to the grease, giving you some idea of the nature of the bottom.

The lead line should be cast ahead of the boat and the marking read when the line is vertical. To find the depth of the water, deduct the distance from your hand to the surface of the water.

Young Samuel Clemens grew up along the Mississippi River where the river pilots had to sound with poles or lead lines in order to follow the shifting channels. He took his pen name, Mark Twain, from the call "By the mark, twain," which means a depth of 2 fathoms as indicated by two strips of leather on the lead line.

A lead line can also be used from a dinghy to sound ahead of your boat to lead you through uncharted waters.

Oar

Don't forget that the trusty oar can be used for sounding if your boat does not have too deep a draft for the length of the oar. When entering an unfamiliar harbor without a detailed chart, you can launch the dinghy and row ahead to sound with an oar.

In some areas, such as in Maine, you often have to contend with hidden rocks in small harbors. Sounding with an oar from your dinghy is advisable if you are not sure of the location of these rocks and suspect your boat might be in danger of striking when it swings at anchor.

Bamboo Pole

Long bamboo poles, painted or notched every foot for sounding, are often found on the decks of boats which ply their trade in areas of shoal or shifting bottoms. You can acquire one of these light, useful poles by either buying a long bamboo fishing pole or keeping an eye peeled for a new rug delivery in the neighborhood. There may be just the bamboo pole for you rolled inside that rug.

16

RDF (Radio Direction Finder)

A **radio direction finder** (generally referred to as an "RDF") is a particular type of radio receiver which picks up signals from transmitting stations called **radiobeacons.** Radiobeacons are located at many strategic navigational aids such as lighthouses, lightships, and towers. Each one transmits a specific characteristic signal. A relative bearing can be taken on radiobeacons by rotating the antenna on an RDF receiver.

Usually, in small radio direction finders, a bar-type antenna across the top of the set pivots from its center. The loudest, or maximum, signal is received by the set when the antenna is rotated so that its long side faces the radiobeacon station. The lowest audible signal, which is called the **null,** is received when the antenna is pointed toward the station.

Beneath the rotating antenna is an azimuth card, or nonmagnetic compass card, printed with 360°. When the antenna is pointed toward the radiobeacon, a relative bearing can be read from the azimuth card and, when added to the magnetic degrees of the ship's heading, gives a bearing on the radiobeacon. A single radio line of position can then be drawn on a chart from the radiobeacon by using the reciprocal of the bearing.

A radiobeacon is identified on nautical charts with a red ring

around the location dot of the navigational aid and it is labeled
'R Bn' for "radiobeacon." There is a radiobeacon at Eastern
Point light on the sample chart. (Eastern Point light is the
57-foot tower on the southern tip of Eastern Point at the
entrance to Gloucester Harbor.) The description following the
abbreviation 'R Bn' means that the RDF frequency for this
radiobeacon is 314 kHz (kiloHertz) and that '. _ . _ & _'
(dot-dash-dot-dash and long dash) is its characteristic, or sound
signal. Most radiobeacons transmit a specific code signal for 48
seconds followed by a 10-second dash.

Radiobeacon transmissions are received on the long-wave,
low-frequency marine band of a radio. Because the space
allotted to marine navigation is small, from 285 kHz to 325
kHz, most of the powerful radiobeacons must share a frequency with other radiobeacons. Radiobeacons on a shared
frequency usually transmit only 1 minute out of a 6-minute
cycle. The portion of this cycle allotted to each radiobeacon,
when its identifying signal may be heard, is given in the *Light
List* (see appendix I). Radiobeacons within a shared frequency
are each given a Roman numeral designation of I through VI,
which shows their sequence of transmission.

Light List Information for an RDF

The "General Information" section of the *Light List*
supplements the information given on a chart for a radiobeacon. A chartlet of a large section of the United States shows
the locations of radiobeacons and they are also listed in the
"Radiobeacon System" list.

The Eastern Point light on the sample chart is listed in
Volume I of the *Light List*. All the radiobeacons on the
Atlantic and Gulf coasts are included in this volume even
though the lights included are limited to those located from

Maine to South Carolina. Information for the Eastern Point radiobeacon frequency is included in the "Radiobeacon System" list as follows.

Freq kHz	Group Sequence	Station	Characteristic	Range (miles)
314	I	MOUNT DESERT	B (– · · ·)	20
	II	MATINICUS ROCK	P (· – – ·)	20
	III	MANANA ISLAND	OE (– – – ·)	100
	IV	HALFWAY ROCK	O (– – –)	20
	V	EASTERN POINT	RT (· – · –)	20
	VI	PORTLAND L.S.	K (– · –)	50

Translated, this means that on frequency 314 kHz on a radio direction finder, on the fifth minute after the hour and every 6 minutes thereafter, the Eastern Point radio station transmits the International Code signal RT (. _ . _). The range of this signal is 20 nautical miles.

The latitude and longitude of each radiobeacon are also given in the list so that they can be located on a chart.

Steps to Operate an RDF

We recommend that you learn to use an RDF, initially by practicing with it in your home and thereafter by frequent use of it on the boat on fair weather days. The latter practice will allow you to check RDF bearings against visually obtained bearings on the same radiobeacons.

1. Line up the RDF or its rotatable azimuth card so that 000° is pointing forward and the 000°–180° axis is parallel to the center line of the boat.

2. Turn on the RDF and rotate the dial on the marine beacon band to the frequency desired.

3. To pick up the desired signal, rotate the RDF antenna so that the signal received is at maximum strength; i.e., the bar antenna should have the long side facing the probable location of the radiobeacon.

4. Without a highly accurate timepiece it is often difficult to determine which radiobeacon time sequence is in operation when the set is turned on initially. Also, some radiobeacons in a sequence are too far away for a signal to be received. Therefore, listen to the first dot-dash character received and identify the radiobeacon and its Roman numeral sequence number in the *Light List,* using either the chartlet or the "Radiobeacon System" list. If this is not the desired beacon, look at your watch to ascertain how many minutes you will have to wait before you will hear the characteristic signal of the radiobeacon in which you are interested.

5. As soon as you hear the proper signal, rotate the antenna 90° and move it back and forth to determine the center of the null (the lowest audible signal). The null indicates the direction of the radiobeacon and often is pinpointed by a visual indicator on an RDF receiver called a **null meter.** If your set does not have a null meter, you must work with the audible signal. Sometimes there is a range in which the signal is blanked out entirely; in this case the center of the silent zone is the null. Finding this center is called "rocking" the antenna. The relative degrees of the null reading are indicated by the position of the antenna over the RDF azimuth card.

6. At the instant the navigator gets the null reading, he calls "Mark!" to the helmsman, who calls back the ship's heading from the ship's compass at that moment. The navigator writes down both the compass and the null reading. (If the ship's compass has not been compensated, the ship's compass heading should be corrected to a

magnetic heading from the ship's compass deviation table.)

7. In order to get the most accurate reading possible, the null reading should now be corrected from an RDF deviation table that has been previously calculated for your RDF. (Directions for making this table are given on page 136.)

8. A null reading is a relative bearing because, as you remember, it is obtained from an azimuth card having the reference degrees in a fixed position relative to the center line of the boat. Therefore, add the corrected ship's magnetic heading (step 6) to this corrected relative bearing (step 7) in order to obtain the magnetic radio bearing on the radiobeacon. If the total degrees exceed 360°, subtract 360° from the figure. You are now ready to go to the chart.

9. Use the reciprocal degrees of the magnetic radio bearing to draw this bearing line on the chart from the location dot of the radiobeacon. (When RDF bearings are taken on radiobeacons which are many miles apart and beyond the limits of a coast chart, they should be plotted on a general chart which covers a greater area.)

10. Write the time the bearing was taken above the radio bearing line and indicate below the line the direction of the bearing from the boat in magnetic degrees followed by the abbreviation 'MAG'.

A second bearing taken on another radiobeacon will give you another line of position. The point where these bearing lines intersect on the chart is marked with a small square, which is labeled with the time the bearings were taken and the letters 'EP' for "estimated position" (as '1030 EP') instead of the 'FIX' used at the intersection of visual bearing lines. Radio bearings are less accurate than visual bearings because any

RDF can be expected to have an error of at least plus or minus 2°, which is more likely to be plus or minus 5° in normal weather. The error may be as much as 10° in rough weather. If land-based radiobeacons are inland, an additional error may be introduced.

When the EP established by RDF bearing lines does not coincide with a course line or DR track, a new course usually is not started at this EP. However, when the EP is an appreciable distance from the course line, we recheck the bearings. If the EP is still the same and if this EP indicates that continuing on our present compass heading would place us in danger, we alter course. Whenever the EP is not on the course line, we take visual bearings on navigational aids as soon as possible. Until we can establish a visual fix, we take RDF bearings at frequent intervals on as many different radiobeacons as possible.

RDF Deviation Table

Upright metal objects aboard a boat, such as stanchions, electrical wires, or rigging, can distort the path of radiobeacon waves. Therefore, a deviation table similar to a ship's compass deviation table should be made up for your RDF.

This is done by locating your boat at a known position and drawing a bearing line on the chart from the boat's position to a charted radiobeacon. Using the compass rose on the chart, determine the magnetic bearing of the radiobeacon.

Rotate your boat at the known position and record magnetic bearings, as they are transmitted by the radiobeacon, for every 15° of the RDF azimuth card starting with 000°. Add each null reading or relative bearing from the RDF to the ship's magnetic heading. These are uncorrected RDF magnetic bearings.

If the number of degrees of the magnetic bearing line drawn

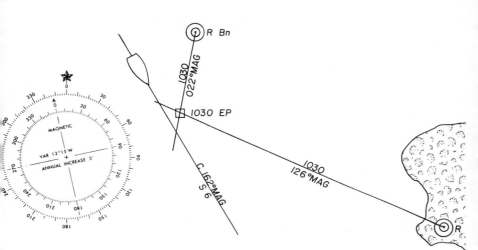

Fig. 22. RDF estimated position.

The intersection of RDF bearing lines is called an estimated position ('EP') since RDF bearings are not considered accurate enough for a fix.

on the chart, as determined from the compass rose, is less than the degrees of the uncorrected RDF magnetic bearings, the difference in degrees is preceded by a minus sign; if the number of degrees is more, the difference is preceded by a plus sign. For example, if the magnetic bearing of a radiobeacon is '150°MAG' on the chart and the uncorrected RDF magnetic bearing is 155°, the deviation correction is −5°.

Corrections of the deviation errors for each relative bearing used on the azimuth card can be plotted on graph paper. Make up the scales on graph paper, using the vertical scale for *correction* in single units from +10° to −10°. The RDF *relative bearings* are marked on the horizontal scale in units of 15° from 000° to 360°. When a line is drawn in a smooth curve through or near the points plotted for the corrections, a cyclical pattern usually will develop, with the curves changing from plus to minus every 90°.

These deviation corrections apply to the RDF only when it is in the same location on the boat as it was at the time the deviation table was made.

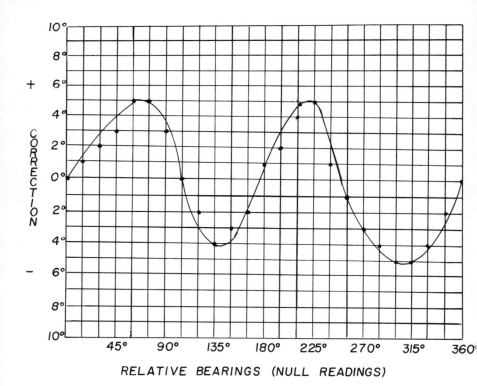

Fig. 23. RDF deviation graph.

Sense Antenna

Some RDF sets have a sense antenna to distinguish the correct bearing from its reciprocal. If your RDF does not have a sense antenna, there is the possibility of being 180° off in your determination of the direction of the radiobeacon because the bearing, as indicated by the null, can be either toward or away from the beacon. Although you will probably have a general idea of the direction of the radiobeacon, if you have any doubt check its position by continuing on course and taking a later bearing on the same radiobeacon. This bearing will intersect the first bearing in the direction of the radio-beacon.

During fog, you may believe you are homing in on, or steering directly toward, an offshore marine radiobeacon, when instead you may be leaving it astern. To check its position, alter course 90° and continue on this course long enough so that a second bearing on this radiobeacon will distinctly intersect your first bearing as drawn on the chart.

Homing

When the steering course is taken from the signal of a radiobeacon, the boat is said to be **homing** on the transmitter. The signal from a radiobeacon is an especially useful navigational aid when cruising out of sight of land, away from other navigational aids, or during times of restricted visibility. In foggy weather the Gloucester fishermen, for example, home in on the Eastern Point radiobeacon when they return with the holds of their trawlers full of fish after several days on the North Atlantic.

It must be mentioned, however, that during times of poor visibility many boats homing on a signal have not only run aground but have rammed the structure housing the radiobeacon. This is one reason why an alert bow watch is always recommended when visibility is poor.

Distance Finding Stations (DFS)

Some lighthouses, lightships, or other navigational aids which have radiobeacons are also **distance finding stations.**

Distance finding stations are located primarily in the New England and Great Lakes sections of the country. They are identified on navigational charts by the initials 'DFS' and on the "Radiobeacon System" chartlet in the *Light List* by a cross through the location circle of the radiobeacon.

Distance finding stations help the navigator determine his distance from the navigational aid in times of decreased visibility. Once every 6 minutes a special 5-second blast of the fog signal on the navigational aid is sounded. It commences at the same instant as the start of the 10-second long dash which is heard on the RDF following the 48-second characteristic signal transmitted from the radiobeacon.

The *Light List* explains distance finding as follows:

> When within audible range of the sound signal, navigators on vessels with radio receivers capable of receiving the radiobeacon signals may readily determine their distance from the station by observing the time in seconds which elapsed between first hearing the beginning of the ten-second radio dash and the beginning of the five-second sound blast and dividing the result by 5.5 for nautical miles. The error of such observations should not exceed 10 percent.
>
> The two seconds of silence preceding the long radio dash is a stand-by or warning signal as is also the one-second fog signal blast. . . .
>
> If the interval between hearing the beginning of the long radio dash marking the end of the radiobeacon minute and the beginning of the long blast of the diaphone is 33 seconds, the observer is $33 \div 5.5 = 6$ miles from the light station.

The speed of a sound, like the blast of a fog signal, changes with the air temperature, and so the figure 5.5 is based on the assumption that the speed of sound is about 1,105 feet per second. It is possible to measure your approximate distance from a radiobeacon in the manner described because one assumes radio sound is received instantaneously.

In the "General Information" section of the *Light List* is an example of the synchronization of sound signals at a DFS with a diaphone fog signal of "1 blast ev 20^s (3^{s}bl)." This fog signal would sound one 3-second blast every 20 seconds for 5 minutes. Our interpretation of their diagram showing how the 5-second fog signal synchronizes with the 10-second radio dash in the sixth minute follows.

R Bn Signal	DFS Fog Signal
48-second dot-dash signal	17-second silence 3-second blast 33-second silence
2-second silence	1-second blast 1-second silence
10-second dash	5-second blast

Aeronautical, AM Radio, and FM Radio Signals

When you can receive aeronautical signals and AM and FM radio frequencies on your RDF, it can also be used to take bearings on aeronautical beacons or on the transmitting antennas of commercial radio stations.

The locations of aeronautical radiobeacons are given in *Sectional Aeronautical Charts.* The latitude and longitude of broadcast stations, which give marine weather forecasts and can be used for RDF bearings, are listed in *Marine Weather Services Charts.* The location of these radiobeacons can be transferred from these charts (see appendix I) to your marine charts.

Automatic Direction Finders

There are sophisticated radio direction finders on the market that automatically register the relative bearing of the station. Tune the set to the desired frequency, and when the dot-dash characteristic is heard an azimuth card rotates automatically to give the relative bearing degrees of the radiobeacon. The card stays in position until another radio station in the group sequence comes on, and then it rotates to give the relative bearing of the new station. The navigator calls "Mark!" to the helmsman as explained in step 6 on page 134. This step and the remaining steps are then followed to determine the magnetic degrees of the radiobeacon bearing.

17

Radar, Loran, Omega, and Omni

WHILE WE DO NOT HAVE THESE ELECTRONIC DEVICES aboard our boats, we have seen them all in operation and mention them for owners of larger boats (or larger pocketbooks). The following discussion will give you some familiarity with these different types of electronic apparatus, an idea of how they work, and a basis for any questions you may wish to ask your marine electronics dealer when you are contemplating a purchase.

Radar

Radar is an instrument which sends out electromagnetic pulses in a narrow beam from an antenna that usually rotates in a complete circle, causing the beam to sweep the horizon. The electromagnetic pulses are reflected back to the antenna from objects, such as buoys and other boats, or from land masses or formations. The reflected pulses are instantly recorded on a circular radarscope, similar to a television screen, with the degrees of the compass marked around the rim. The pulses are converted on the radarscope to blips, or patches of light. The scene, so to speak, is viewed as if from a point directly above the boat, with the boat located in the center of the screen. The blips last for a short time, then disappear as the beam continues its sweep of the horizon, only to reappear in each return sweep.

As most commercial ships are equipped with radar, it is important during fog for cruising boats to have radar reflectors placed as high as possible on the boat. However, even with this precaution, it must be realized that radar sets usually have a minimum range of about 30 yards under which the set cannot record objects. Persons aboard small cruising boats that are socked in by thick fog find this shortcoming alarming when they are overwhelmed by the ear-splitting fog signals of a ferryboat or ship which seems to be bearing down on them. At a moment like this, they take small comfort in the possibility that the radar operator has picked them up earlier on his radarscope.

The distance between blips and the boat can be determined on the radarscope. The magnetic bearing of an object can be computed by adding the relative bearing determined from the rim of the radarscope to the ship's magnetic heading. These features make it easy to get lines of position or a fix from a radar set.

Lines of position and radar fixes can be established in several ways, such as by a bearing line with the distance off marked on it, by two bearings taken on either side of a small island along with a circle of distance from a structure on the island, or by three bearings. A radar fix established by the intersection of two circles of distance from two structures is considered to be the most accurate fix, because the distance from a structure determined from the radarscope is more reliable than the relative bearing to the structure. A radar fix is marked with a small circle, the time of the sighting, and the abbreviation 'RAD FIX'. When navigational aids are equipped with radar reflectors, they are identified on the charts with the abbreviation 'RA REF'.

New owners of radar sets should practice with them often under conditions of good visibility to become familiar with interpreting the blips on the radarscope. This is the time to experiment in establishing fixes by the several methods available, to discover the minimum range of a particular set, and to compare the lesser accuracy of radar bearings with more reliable visual bearings.

Portable Radar

The *Whistler* (Kimball Products Company, Inc., P.O. Box 343, Sudbury, Massachusetts 01776) is a compact portable radar set which differs from conventional radar equipment in that it has no radarscope; its prime signal is received audibly. An adjustable strap is worn around the operator's neck and supports the 5-pound set slightly above the waist.

Elaborate installation is unnecessary because the boat's 12-volt system or a portable 12-volt battery pack serves as its power source. A rotating antenna is also unnecessary because the operator, after slipping his hands through the hand straps on each side of the set, scans the horizon with the front of the set. As objects come into range, a signal is received through lightweight earphones. In addition to the audible signal, a meter on the top of the set displays the distance of the object. We were told that this meter can be used for distances up to one mile.

The higher the pitch of the signal received, the farther away the object. During our Whistler practice session at Boston Harbor, we noted that a land mass a little over 2 miles away produced a comparatively steady high tone. As the set was

moved to pick up intervening buoys, a shrill whistle or warble
was heard as each buoy was brought into range. The signal
received from buoys equipped with radar reflectors was
unmistakable and particularly strong and shrill. The closer an
object is, the lower the tone of the signal. With practice, we
began to interpret from the tone of the signal an approxima-
tion of the distance of a buoy from our location. Passing
powerboats were easily identifiable by a burbling sound
somewhat similar to that of the engine of a boat.

The maximum operational range of the Whistler is said to be
2 miles on a shoreline, up to ½ mile on a small boat or buoy, up
to 1 mile on a large boat or buoy, and up to 1½ miles on a
radar reflector; the minimum range is 50 feet from the unit.

We were told that the Whistler is waterproofed against rain
and salt spray. It has received type approval for operation
under Part 83 of the Federal Communications Commission
(FCC) rules. According to the manufacturer of the Whistler,
the FCC rules "require a minimum of a station license and one
person aboard with a restricted radiotelephone operator's
license (permit). If you already have these licenses for a
radiotelephone, you need only obtain an endorsement to your
station license from the FCC."

The compactness and low cost (under $700) of the Whistler
should recommend it to many yachtsmen. We believe it has
merit. However, we required about 30 minutes' practice
before we were able to sort out the different sounds and match
them with the objects from which they originated. We would
also want considerably more practice before we would be
willing to trust our interpretations in a fog. We understand,
however, that persons with musical training distinguish between the tones much more rapidly than we were able to.

Loran

Loran is a type of radio receiving set with which lines of position can be obtained from pairs of loran transmitting stations. Each pair of stations consists of a master station and a slave station. The signals received by the set are adjusted by the operator so that the set can measure the time difference between pulses from the two stations.

Most coast and general charts have loran lines printed on them. (Note the green, red, and yellow loran lines drawn on the sample chart.) The measured time difference (a four-digit number) is compared with the four-digit numbers printed on the loran lines. When the time difference numbers do not fall directly on a loran line, the navigator must estimate or interpolate the locations of the line of position between two loran lines in order to draw it on a chart.

A line of position obtained from a second master transmitter and its slave transmitter establishes a fix at the point where it intersects the first line of position. The fix is identified with a small circle which is labeled with the time the fix was established and the words 'LORAN FIX'.

Loran has several advantages. It is compact and easy to install; there are many loran stations along the coasts of the United States; and loran fixes over most of the coastal waters are claimed to be accurate within $1\frac{1}{8}$ miles in a 500-mile range.

Omega

When the Omega navigation system is in full operation, navigators will be able to get a fix anyplace in the world at any time of the day or night. The accuracy of the fix is said to be within about 500 feet to 1 mile in the daytime and 2 miles at night, even when a boat is 6,000 miles from either or both of the transmitting stations.

A total of eight transmitting stations comprise the Omega system. They are placed strategically around the globe. The first four, which were used successfully for several years of experimentation, were built in Norway, Trinidad, Hawaii, and New York. The Norway transmitting station is referred to as "A," the Trinidad station as "B," the Hawaiian station as "C," and the New York station as "D." The system will be completed with the construction of the remaining four stations in New Zealand, Australia, Madagascar, and Japan. Once these stations are constructed, the New York station will be moved to North Dakota.

Omega signals can be received from a great distance because they are transmitted in the very low frequency (VLF) band between 10 and 14 kHz. VLF frequencies are not greatly influenced by weather or night effect. They also penetrate about 40 feet into salt water and can therefore be picked up by submarines.

Omega stations transmit on three VLF frequencies, one of which is a basic frequency of 10.2 kHz. The stations repeat a 10-second sequence of signals, and the network transmitters are controlled by atomic clocks. The sequences are interrelated among the eight Omega stations so that only one station transmits on a specific frequency at one time, for approximately 1 second during each 10-second interval. A receiving set aboard a boat measures the distances from two selected transmitting stations and displays this information.

According to a pilot chart published by the U.S. Naval Oceanographic Office, "vertical whip antennas 20–30 feet in height are generally used for shipboard installations." It is not necessary to have three antennas to bring in the three VLF frequencies, the Naval Oceanographic Office states, because of "the development of multifrequency antenna couplers."

To use Omega, the navigator selects a pair of transmitting stations, such as "A" and "C" (Norway and Hawaii), on the basic Omega frequency of 10.2 kHz. The receiving set receives electromagnetic signals from "A" and "C" and determines the phase relationship of their signals. An indication of this relationship is displayed by the receiver. The navigator corrects this information for changes in the ionosphere layers in the earth's atmosphere by referring to a skywave correction table. He then plots a single line of position (LOP) on an Omega chart. (Charts drawn in the Mercator projection are used for Omega.) The skywave correction table and Omega charts are published by the U.S. Naval Oceanographic Office.

A second single LOP is determined between another pair of transmitting stations such as "B" and "C" (Trinidad and Hawaii). The second pair should be selected to give an LOP as nearly perpendicular to the first LOP as possible. When this second LOP is plotted on the chart, the fix where the LOP lines cross is labeled 'OMEGA FIX'.

The Omega system can be described by comparing waves of water to electromagnetic waves. When this analogy is used, the assumption is that the crests of the waves are of equal height, the troughs are of equal depth, and the wave crests remain a fixed distance apart.

If you drop a stone into an absolutely still pond of water, ever-increasing circles of waves will spread out from the point where the stone enters the water. If another stone of the same size is dropped far away in this pond, an identical circular wave pattern develops. When the two patterns of waves meet each other, each circular wave will intersect another in two places as they move along their way. Not only do the crests of waves moving toward each other intersect, but so do their troughs. The waves are considered to be in phase at the points where they intersect, and a line connecting points of intersection is referred to as a **zero phase difference line.**

On the frequency 10.2 kHz, the electromagnetic waves sent out from each Omega transmitting station are 16 miles apart. As zero phase occurs twice in each wave, the distance between each two zero phase difference lines is 8 miles on the direct line between any pair of transmitting stations. The area bounded by adjacent zero phase difference lines is referred to as a **lane** in Omega language. These lanes become wider and wider the farther a boat moves away from the direct line between the two stations.

Incidents of zero phase difference develop a curved pattern which when depicted as lines on a chart is called a **hyperbolic system.** On charts which we would use for navigation, however, the curvature of the lines is not noticeable. Each zero phase difference line on the Omega chart is identified by the letters of the pair of selected Omega stations, and an international convention for numbering the lines from one of the stations to the other has been established.

For example, when using stations "A" and "C" (Norway and Hawaii), one line on an Omega chart could be identified by 'AC 540' and the next 'AC 543', illustrating that from the station in Norway there would be 540 and 543 zero phase lines. The grid of lines on the Omega chart enables a navigator to select the best combinations of stations that give him a good fix.

Before leaving a port, an Omega receiver should be set for the lane which includes this port. The receiver should be left on during the day's run; there is a counter in the receiver which automatically counts the zero phase difference lines as they are crossed.

By comparing the signals from the two selected stations, the receiver reads out on a dial the percentage of the distance between adjacent zero phase difference lines which has been traversed. This information is corrected by using the skywave correction table. When this corrected figure is added to the lane counter figure, the result is the number used to chart an LOP.

For example, if the lane counter for "AC" shows 541, the dial reads 63, and the correction from the skywave correction table is − 12, then the LOP is 'AC 541.63' minus .12, or 'AC 541.51'. A line then can be plotted on the Omega chart 51 percent, or about midway, between 'AC 540' and 'AC 543'.

The same procedure is used for another pair of stations. Two different stations can be selected, or one of the first stations can be used with a new station.

The lane counter cannot be used continuously aboard boats under sail alone because the 12-volt system cannot tolerate the approximately 7-ampere drain for very long. When not in use, it is usually possible to determine the lane from a DR track plotted on a chart during the run.

If the receiver is also equipped with the other two frequencies used by Omega stations, 11.33 and 13.6 kHz, the operator can use these frequencies to see if he is using the correct lane. Since all the transmitting stations send out signals on these two frequencies as well as on the basic 10.2-kHz frequency, the three frequencies are synchronized in the 10-second sequence. The additional information received from 13.6 kHz makes it possible to identify the correct lane if the position of the boat is known within 24 miles; the 11.33-kHz frequency makes it possible to identify the lane if the position of the boat is known within 72 miles.

Prices of Omega sets vary from more than $20,000 for highly sophisticated sets for military use to under $5,000 for sets equipped with only the 10.2-kHz frequency. We hope the price of an Omega receiver becomes lower; we believe this navigational system is invaluable, particularly for cruising offshore or in fog or other conditions of restricted visibility. The fixes are arrived at easily in any kind of weather, and the machine does almost all the calculation.

Omni (Omnirange Direction Finding System)

The omnirange direction finding system has long been an important navigational aid for aircraft, and "omni" sets are also manufactured for installation aboard cruising boats. Because omnirange signals follow a line-of-sight course, the height of the receiver antenna is one factor that determines the range of reception; this limits its use for marine navigation. However, the reception aboard boats is likely to be satisfactory when the antenna is 25 to 30 feet above the water and the boat is within 20 miles of an omni station.

Omnirange stations operate within the band of 112–118 mHz, and each station is identified by either a three-letter Morse code or a voice recording.

In a simplified way, the principle of omni can be compared to a lighthouse using both a 360° all-around light, which radiates in all directions, and a beam of light rotating at a specific rate. The 360° light flashes each time the beam passes through magnetic north. The elapsed time between the sighting of the flash of light and the sighting of the beam can be counted to determine a bearing from the lighthouse. For example, if the narrow beam makes a complete revolution every minute, an observer knows that he is on a bearing of 180° magnetic when he sees a flash of light 30 seconds after he spots the narrow beam of light.

In place of the 360° flashing light, the omnirange station sends out bearings 360° around the station at 1° intervals. A second signal is rotated around the station. The difference between the two signals is measured electronically by an omni receiving set, and a magnetic bearing is indicated on a dial.

Magnetic bearings are recorded either *to* or *from* the omnirange station, depending on the direction selected for the to/from indicator. When using the instrument aboard a boat for a single bearing, the indicator should be in the "from" position in order to be able to plot this bearing more easily on the chart.

The locations of omnirange stations can be identified in *Sectional Aeronautical Charts* (see appendix I) by a rectangular blue outline which boxes the name of the airport, the station frequency, and other transmitting identification. A magnetic compass rose surrounds each station. Omnirange stations are further identified by the letters 'VOR' or 'VORTAC' on sectional charts. 'VOR' means "very high frequency omnidirectional radio range." 'VORTAC' is a combination of the abbreviations VOR and TACAN ("ultrahigh frequency tactical air navigational aid").

An omni set equipped with a VOR receiver can use both VOR and VORTAC for bearings. When an omni set is also equipped with TACAN, it registers the distance of the omnirange station in nautical miles. This combination provides an automatic fix. However, we have seen omni sets equipped only for taking bearings; these are remarkably accurate for establishing fixes whenever there are two omnirange stations within 20 miles of the boat and there is no hill or other obstruction between the station and the boat.

To be useful for coastal navigation, the latitude and longitude of the omni stations in your cruising area should be measured on aeronautical charts and marked on nautical charts. An omni fix is marked on the chart with a small circle, the time of the fix, and the words 'OMNI FIX'.

18

Current

Tidal Current is constantly being confused with the rise and fall of the tide. Although it is related to tidal changes, current is only the *horizontal* movement of the water. A change in the direction of its flow rarely coincides exactly with the time of either high or low tide because of the ragged contour of the shoreline.

In our estimation, current is responsible for more missed seamarks or landfalls than any other factor. Ashore, when you go a certain distance in a specific direction you can be assured of arriving at a specific destination, if there is no mishap. Not so on the water. Although a skipper may steer a very accurate compass course, the body of water itself is often moving insidiously in one direction or another and taking the boat along with it.

Current is described according to the direction and speed of its flow. The direction toward which the water is flowing is called **set** and is expressed in true degrees. For example, if a current is running from the east toward the west, the set will be 270°. The velocity, or speed, at which the water is flowing is called **drift** and is expressed in knots and tenths of knots, such as 2.5 knots. The drift therefore is the number of nautical

154

miles the current would carry a floating object in one hour, ignoring the action of wind and waves.

In many situations, a navigator can use a government booklet entitled *Tidal Current Tables* to help him determine the action of the current and the probable influence it will exert on his boat.

Tidal Current Tables

In the *Tidal Current Tables* (see appendix I), **slack water** indicates 0.0 knot of current; **maximum current** is its greatest velocity for each area during one cycle. The general direction of the current when it is flowing into harbors and bays is called **flood;** when it is flowing out, it is called **ebb.** To interpret the predictions, you must be familiar with twenty-four–hour time (see page 61), which is used in these tables.

Two volumes of the *Tidal Current Tables,* one for the Atlantic Coast and one for the Pacific Coast, are published annually. Predictions of the time, true direction, and velocity of current for each day of the year are given for reference stations. These predictions are the basis for calculating the current for subordinate stations. The stations are arranged in geographical order. Excellent directions for using the tables precede each table.

Table 1 gives daily predictions for slack water and maximum current at reference stations like Boston Harbor (Deer Island light), or the Savannah River entrance (between jetties). Table 2 gives information on current for many locations along the coastline; these locations are called "subordinate stations" and are identified by name, latitude, and longitude. By using table 3, it is possible to calculate the approximate velocity of the current for any time between slack water and maximum current.

The tables should be consulted to determine the effect the current may have on the boat, particularly in canals, straits, and rivers. For example, at Hellgate in the East River of New York City, the eddies at maximum current can cause a cruising boat to whirl out of control. Because the maximum current is sometimes more than 5 knots, we schedule our trips through Hellgate near slack water and the majority of the trip on the East River with a favorable current.

Whenever there is a strong wind blowing against a strong current, steep and choppy waves build up, making passage extremely difficult. This is a condition often encountered in long bays with strong currents, like Delaware Bay, and in narrow cuts with strong currents, like the entrance to Miami Harbor. When you are faced with this, it is a good idea to consult the *Tidal Current Tables* to find out the time of a weaker current; otherwise wait either for the wind to subside or for the wind and current to be with you.

Unfortunately, these tables are based on waters adjacent to land, and although helpful they do not provide the navigator with enough information when he is even a few miles offshore. There are areas, however, where surveys have been made of tidal currents farther out; these findings are available in a publication called *Tidal Current Charts*.

Tidal Current Charts

Tidal Current Charts (see appendix I) are provided for some major boating areas where the set and drift of the current varies considerably as it flows through narrow passages between islands and around fingers of land projecting into harbors, bays, and sounds. The set of the current is shown by arrows, and the drift by the number of knots. *Tidal Current Charts* do not have to be renewed each year because they are based on the time predictions at reference stations in *Tidal Current Tables*, which are published annually.

Estimating Set and Drift

When *Tidal Current Charts* are not available for a cruising area, you can estimate the set and drift of the current by watching the buildup of water on one side of a buoy and the path of the wake on the other side. For instance, we judge a little rippled wake to indicate a drift of about half a knot, but when a buoy is pushed over so the water churns up and around it, the drift is likely to be more than 2 knots. When there are no buoys present, you can estimate the set and drift of the current by observing the action of the water around lobster pots, stakes, or other stationary objects.

Commercial boatmen have learned by experience the general directions of the flood and ebb of the current in their area, and you can glean a great deal of local knowledge through conversations with them.

When you are cruising along a coast past the entrances to long bays, as is often the case in Maine, the effect of the flood and ebb of the current can noticeably affect the direction in which your boat travels. Sometimes the effect of the current of large bays is felt several miles at sea.

Estimating Course and Speed

Since set and drift are given in true degrees in the *Tidal Current Tables*, we work out problems concerned with current in true degrees—but place the compass degrees of a course in parentheses after them such as '(C 102°C)'.

To estimate your time of arrival at a destination with a reasonable degree of accuracy, determine the effect any appreciable current has on your boat as it travels to that destination. It is a comparatively simple matter to determine the effect of current when the set is either the same as your course or 180° from your course.

For example, assume the course is '090° (C 102°C)', the boat speed is 6 knots, the set is 270°, and the average drift for the time of your trip is 2 knots. Because the current is setting the boat back along its course at 2 miles each hour, the speed over the ground (labeled 'SOG') is only 4 knots, and in one hour the boat will travel 4 miles.

When the current is at an angle to your course, the calculations become more complex. In this case, it is necessary to determine the proper compass course to steer in order to stay on a track to your destination.

When working with current (as illustrated in Fig. 25), the line drawn on a chart from one navigational aid to another is called a **track** instead of a course. A track is labeled above the line with the true degrees of its direction preceded by the letters 'TR' for "track."

The true degrees to the destination, from which the compass course is determined, differs from the true degrees of the track because of the set of the current. Thus, the course steered compensates for the effect of the current on the boat's path through the water and enables the boat to remain on the track to the destination, even though it moves crablike through the water.

A current line to show the set is plotted from the track in the direction the water is flowing. This is the direction a boat without power would move if it were floating with the current. The word 'SET' and the true direction in degrees is written above this line.

The length of the current line is determined by the velocity of the current, which is expressed as knots of drift. Since knots

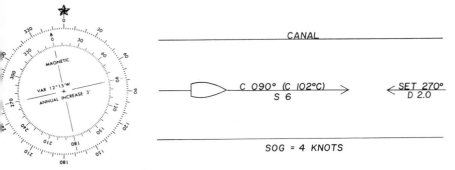

Fig. 24. Current 180° from course.

(True degrees are used in calculations for current because the *Tidal Current Tables* give the direction of the current in true degrees.)

Course: 090° true (102° compass).

Speed: 6 knots.

Set: 270° true.

Drift: 2.0 knots.

SOG (speed over ground) of boat: 4 knots (in this case, boat speed minus drift).

represent nautical miles traveled in one hour, this figure can be measured with dividers on the latitude scale of a chart and the measurement applied to the current line. The letter 'D' for "drift" followed by the averaged speed in one hour is written below the current line.

The drift of the current for the time you expect to be affected by it is averaged so that the computed compass course for steering, and the speed of the boat over the ground, can be assumed to be constant for the length of the track.

The word **course** is reserved for a line drawn from the end of the current line to the track, according to the measurement of the boat speed. The direction of this line, which is the direction a boat must be steered to stay on the track to its destination, is written above the line in true degrees preceded by the letter 'C' for "course." The compass course is placed in parentheses and is written as '(C°C)'. As the length of the course line is determined by the boat speed, this speed is written below the line preceded by the letter 'S' for "speed."

When a boat is being affected by current, the boat speed

(the speed it makes through the water as shown by a speed indicator) is not the speed the boat is making over the ground. This speed over the ground, depending on the direction of the set and the strength of the drift of the current, may be more or less than the boat's speed through the water. **Speed over the ground** is written as 'SOG' on the chart below the track line.

One hour is the easiest unit of time used in making the calculations for current, so that the distance traveled in one hour and the boat speed in knots will be the same figure.

The following example shows a method of calculating and plotting that allows for the effect of current when it is at an angle to the boat.

Track from 'N "2"' to 'GONG "14"': 090°.
Boat speed through water: 6 knots.
Set of current: 120°.
Average drift of current expected for duration of trip from 'N "2"' to 'GONG "14"': 2.0 knots.

1. Draw a line connecting 'N "2"' and 'GONG "14"'. Above this line write 'TR 090°'. The beginning of the track at 'N "2"' is labeled 'A' and the end of the track at 'GONG "14"' is labeled 'B'.

2. From 'A', draw the current line 120°, which is the set of the current. Above the line write 'SET 120°'.

3. From 'A', use a drawing compass to mark off on the current line 2.0 miles, which represents the 2.0 nautical miles per hour (knots) of the drift. Label the point where this mark intersects the current line 'X'. Below the line, write 'D 2.0' for the drift.

4. Extend the drawing compass to a measurement of 6 miles, for the 6 knots of boat speed, and place one leg on 'X'. Make a mark on the track line and label this intersection 'Y'.

5. Draw a line from 'X' to 'Y'. Determine the true

degrees of this line; label 'C 080° (C 094°C)' above the line and 'S 6' below the line. The compass course in parentheses is the information the skipper will use to steer to 'GONG "14" '.

6. Convert 080° of the course line to a compass course by using the "True Virgins Conversion Steps." (If your ship's compass is compensated, magnetic degrees can be used.) Assume, for this problem, the variation is '12°W' and the deviation is '2°W', giving you a compass course of 'C 094°C'. Write the compass course in parentheses after the true course, since these are the degrees to be used for steering.

7. Use the dividers to measure the distance on the track from 'A' to 'Y'. This measurement will be the average speed over the ground as well as the average mileage traveled in one hour along the track to 'GONG "14" '. Speed over the ground is written below the track line as 'SOG 7.6'.

The speed made good over the ground is used to work out speed/time/distance problems, such as the estimated time of arrival at 'GONG "14" ' for this problem. Use your dividers to measure the track from 'Y' to 'GONG "14" ', which is 4.5 miles, and use this with the SOG figure in the following formula:

$$\frac{D \times 60}{S} = T$$

$\frac{4.5 \times 60}{7.6} = \underline{34}$ minutes estimated time from 'Y' to 'GONG "14" '

Therefore, it should take *1 hour and 34 minutes* to reach 'GONG "14" ' after passing 'N "2" '. (The initial calculations are based on the time of one hour from 'A' ('N "2" ') to 'Y', and this is added to the answer, 34 minutes, to find the ETA at 'GONG "14" '.

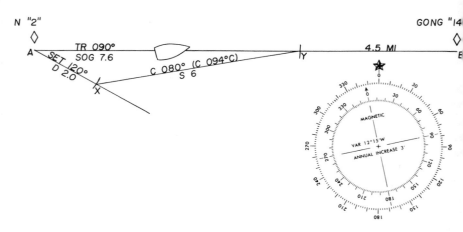

Fig. 25. Current at angle to track.

(One hour is the unit of time used for calculation.)

Track line AB ('TR'): 090° true (boat's path through water).

Current line AX: 120° of set (true direction of current) drawn from track.

    (2.0 knots of drift = 2 miles from 'A' to 'X'; drawn with a compass. The drift figure is averaged.)

Course line XY: 6 miles (because boat speed = 6 knots); drawn with a compass.

    (Steering course = 094° compass, assuming a 2°W deviation: $T = 080°, V = 12°W, M = 092°, D = 2°W, C = 094°$. By steering this course, the boat will crab along the track as it compensates for the effect of the current.)

SOG (speed over ground): 7.6 knots (mileage measurement of line AY).

    This speed is used to determine ETA (estimated time of arrival) at 'GONG "14"'. (YB = 4.5 miles.)

$$\frac{D \times 60}{S} = T \qquad \frac{4.5 \times 60}{7.6} = 34 \text{ minutes}$$

Total travel time from 'N "2"' to 'GONG "14"': 1 hour 34 minutes.

We prefer to work out the effect of current on a separate sheet of paper instead of on the chart, since this calculation will not be used again. The solutions to these one-time problems are entered in the log book. This keeps erasures on the chart at a minimum.

When working on a separate sheet of paper, a circular protractor is used as a compass rose. A dot is placed on the paper to indicate the navigational aid 'N "2" ' in the example. The center of the circular protractor is placed on this dot; marks are made on the paper at 090° for the true degrees of the track, and at 120° for the true degrees of the set. Parallel rulers are used as a straightedge to draw the track, the set line, and so forth, as described above.

19

Leeway

THE ACTION OF THE WIND blowing against the side of a hull can cause a boat to diverge from the intended track; it must be allowed for in addition to any allowance made for current. The stronger the velocity of the wind, the more it will cause your boat to diverge from its course. The angle between the intended track and the actual track of a moving boat, as caused by this wind action, is called **leeway**.

Leeway is dramatically illustrated by the sideslip or crablike movement of a sailboat attempting to sail close to the wind with the centerboard raised. Powerboats and sailboats are making leeway when the disturbed water or trail of bubbles in the wake angles off to the side. When there is a current and no leeway is being made, the wake of a boat will stream out directly behind, because the current carries the boat and its wake at the same rate.

A rough estimate of leeway can be made by towing the rotator of a taffrail log off the stern of the boat. Because it rotates below the surface of the water, the rotator is not affected by the wind and tends to follow a straight line, whereas a boat, which is affected by the wind, tends to crab along. Therefore, the angle of leeway can be seen by how much the line of the taffrail log slues to one side of the projected center line of the boat.

To correct for leeway, the course must be altered toward the wind the same number of degrees as the angle made by either the wake or the taffrail log line from the projected center line of the boat.

20

Tides

Tide REFERS to the daily *vertical rise and fall* of the waters of the ocean. This phenomenon can vary considerably depending upon your location. The tide is a negligible consideration, for instance, in Chesapeake Bay, where the range of the tide is usually about 1 to 2 feet. In Massachusetts Bay, however, the average tide is about 9 feet. In the Bay of Fundy, Nova Scotia, the tidal range varies from 20 feet to more than 40 feet at different times during the year.

Tide is influenced by the position of the moon in relation to the sun, with the moon having the greater influence. The average length of a lunar, or tidal, day is about 24 hours 50 minutes; it is thus longer than the solar day by which we reckon our time. There are usually two high tides and two low tides each day, but since the tidal cycle occurs about 50 minutes later on each succeeding day, one tide may skip to the next day.

Tide Tables

The *Tide Tables* (see appendix I) for North America, like the *Tidal Current Tables*, are published in two volumes, one for the East Coast and one for the West Coast. Daily predictions for the times and heights of high and low waters are given for reference stations. These predictions are the basis for calculating the tides for subordinate stations. The stations are arranged in geographical order. Excellent directions for using the tables precede each table.

Table 1 gives daily predictions for high and low tides for areas like Boston or Savannah, which are used as reference stations. Table 2 gives tidal information for many locations along the coastline; these locations are called "subordinate stations" and are identified by name, latitude, and longitude. By using table 3, it is possible to calculate the height of the water for any time between high and low tide. These predictions are given in twenty-four–hour time (see page 61).

The mean low water soundings printed on the Atlantic and Gulf coast charts, on which the figures in the *Tide Tables* are based, refer to an average of the low tides for an area. The mean lower low soundings on the Pacific Coast charts refer to an average of the lowest of the two daily low tides.

To find the depth of the water for a specific time and place, the number of feet determined from the *Tide Tables* must be added to or subtracted from the soundings on the charts.

By referring to the *Tide Tables*, you can choose a safe time for taking a short cut across shoal waters or for exploring harbors with shoal entrances. For example, in the Abaco Islands in the Bahamas, the entrances to many beautiful harbors are so shallow that entry at the time of low water is denied to boats with a draft of more than 5 feet.

Refer to the *Tide Tables* before choosing a place to anchor in an unfamiliar harbor where the tidal range is appreciable; this will assure you of a level bunk for the entire night. One night of sleeping on a tilt with your boat high and dry will show you the wisdom of this move.

Sometimes the height of your boat is close to the clearance indicated for a fixed bridge. Because heights of structures above the water are given on the charts in feet above mean high water, reference to the *Tide Tables* makes it possible to time your arrival to pass under the bridge at low tide. Mean high water is given for a few key areas in the 'Tidal Information' table on harbor and coast charts.

Estimating the Tide

The range of the tide can be estimated roughly by noting the high water mark on rocks and pilings as well as banks and beaches along the shore. If you hear a weather report or overhear comments ashore of unusually high tides, caution should be exercised before anchoring in shoal harbors or cruising shoal water areas. When the moon is full or new, the range of the tide is likely to increase; these tides are called **spring tides.**

Water Level Fluctuations in the Great Lakes

Although the Great Lakes are not tidal, their water level is likely to change from year to year as well as several times within any one year. To help the mariner determine these depth changes, the *Monthly Bulletin of Lake Levels* and the supplements to the *Great Lakes Pilot* (see appendix I) report the inches each lake is above (" + ") or below (" − ") the 'Low Water Datum' figure of the soundings printed on the charts. In addition, they include a forecast of the differences expected during the latter part of a month. In general, each month the average change in the levels of the different lakes varies from 1 to 3 feet, and the average difference during the entire year is about 4 to 6 feet. The lowest water in the Great Lakes during the navigating season occurs during the spring and fall, and these are the seasons of the greatest storm activity.

The levels of the Great Lakes are also temporarily influenced by storms and winds, and the changes may last for several hours. In its "General Description of Lake Erie," the *Great Lakes Pilot* notes that "the lake level is affected . . . by strong winds of sustained speed and direction which drive the surface water forward to raise its level on the lee shore and lower it on the weather shore. This type of fluctuation has a very pronounced effect on Lake Erie, because it is the shallowest of the Great Lakes." These conditions also prevail on Lake Huron, Lake Michigan, and Lake Superior. However, the *Great Lakes Pilot* has this to say about Lake Ontario: "The great depth materially limits the fluctuations of level due to wind, rendering them comparatively small."

21

Fog

NAVIGATING IN A FOG, a driving rainstorm, or any condition of restricted visibility can be a disconcerting experience if you have not prepared for it ahead of time. The skills necessary for navigating in a fog should be second nature; practice them frequently in clear weather. The time to experiment with the navigational equipment aboard is not under foggy conditions, as is sometimes done by yachtsmen who rely on visual or "church steeple" navigation in clear weather.

It is a good habit to check compass directions frequently whenever you are under way. Whenever you see a low fog bank along the horizon or notice that the outlines or shapes on shore are becoming hazy, establish your position immediately by taking several bearings on charted objects before they are lost to sight. A lookout should also be stationed on the bow as soon as the visibility lessens.

Plotting a DR (dead reckoning) track and keeping a well-documented ship's log book should be practiced in clear weather: use all the information available from the compass, RDF, depth sounder, and any other navigational equipment aboard. As more than one person aboard should be familiar with the problems which have to be faced when navigating in fog, this clear-weather practicing offers a relaxed atmosphere for learning. On long cruises, it is an interesting project for everyone in the family and will also be of interest to guests.

Reduced Speed

The time-proven procedure to follow in fog is to reduce the speed of a boat so that it is possible to stop within half the distance of visibility. This usually means a very slow speed, but it is the only safe way to operate under this condition. It must be remembered, however, when following a course that the slower the boat is moving, the more effect the current will have on its track.

Fog Signals *(Rules of the Road)*

All yachtsmen should be familiar with the required fog signals, which are listed in *Rules of the Road: International-Inland*; *Rules of the Road: Great Lakes*; and *Rules of the Road: Western Rivers* (see appendix I), published by the U.S. Coast Guard. We urge you to keep aboard for reference a copy of the book that covers your waters.

A few of the Rules for boats under power or sail at times of low visibility follow.

Powerboats under way:
Inland—*one prolonged* blast, 4 to 6 seconds long, at least every minute.
International—*one prolonged* blast, 4 to 6 seconds long, at least every 2 minutes.
Great Lakes—distinct blasts at least every minute.
Sailboats under way, short blasts at least every minute:
Starboard tack—*one* blast every minute.

Port tack—*two* blasts in succession every minute.

Wind abaft the beam—*three* blasts in succession every minute.

Any vessel at anchor in a fairway:

International/Inland—a bell rung rapidly for a period of about 5 seconds at least every minute.

Great Lakes—a bell rung rapidly for a period of 3 to 5 seconds at least every 2 minutes; in addition, a signal of one short blast, two long blasts, and one short blast in quick succession at intervals of not more than 3 minutes.

Radar Reflector

A small, compact radar reflector should be aboard every cruising boat and can be purchased for a few dollars at most nautical supply stores. It is usually required by race committees for participants in offshore sailing races which take place across open water or extend overnight. Lightweight radar reflectors are opened and hung in the rigging during times of restricted visibility. As wood and fiberglass are difficult to pick up on a radarscope, these reflectors serve as an important safety feature. An aluminum mast cannot be depended upon to act as a reflector because the waves sent out by a radar set tend to be deflected by a curved object, instead of bouncing back to the set in order to record it on the radarscope.

A radar reflector can be improvised by either lashing cooking utensils to the rigging or using sheets of aluminum foil. Both jury rigs should be placed to reflect in at least two planes.

Listening for Sounds

The distance at which a fog horn may be heard is influenced by atmospheric conditions and is unpredictable. Sometimes distant sounds can be heard loudly in fog, but there are times when you may hear the signal faintly or not at all even though the navigational aid actually is close at hand. When a boat is under power, it is advisable to shut off the motor from time to time to listen for the audible navigational aids. The navigator should tell crew members when to alert their ears and eyes to locate a navigational aid which, according to his DR track, should be within hearing distance and perhaps even visible. Even when the aid is just heard and not seen, it could be entered in the log book, for example, as "1253 heard BELL "14" abeam to port."

One way to have confidence in the direction of an audible buoy is to have some of the persons aboard close their eyes in order to concentrate on the sound and then point in the direction from which they hear it. In practice, we have found everyone usually points in the same direction. Pointing the wide end of a megaphone toward the sound and holding the small end to your ear often helps to magnify the sound. Despite the poor visibility, binoculars will often help you locate a buoy before it is visible to the naked eye.

Mariners in the past, who lacked our advantage of so many audible navigational aids, would listen for shore sounds as they approached land, such as crowing roosters, twittering birds, and in particular barking dogs. Interestingly enough, this was referred to as "dog-bark navigation" because the sound of barking dogs seemed to carry a longer distance in fog than the other sounds mentioned. Usually it was the first indication of land on a fogbound coast.

When there is a sea running, we listen for the sound of

breaking surf. Even small wavelets make a discernible sound when splashing on exposed rocks or sandy banks.

Lighthouse Fog Signals

Fog signals function during times of restricted visibility. The noise characteristics of the signals at fixed stations or at lighthouses are described in the *Light List* (see appendix I). Sometimes when you are socked in by fog, you feel the rest of the world must be too. Often, however, your fogbound situation does not cover a very great area, and you cannot always count on the fog signal at a nearby lighthouse being in operation—because the sun may be shining brightly there. In addition, more and more lighthouses are being operated mechanically, which is not as reliable as the continuous watch maintained by resident personnel.

You should also be alert to the fact that sound is tricky and can be deflected by a high jut of land. Therefore, although fog signals usually can be heard at a great distance, they can be inaudible in certain areas where there is an intervening land mass, even when the location of the signal is not far away.

In times of low visibility, it is often important for a navigator to be able to differentiate between the sounds of a fog-signaling device from a navigational aid and the fog signals of nearby boats that cannot be seen. Following are our interpretations of sound signals most commonly used on lighthouses and lightships.

1. A **diaphone** makes a slow, mournful sound. It is usually a two-toned *bee-bah,* but sometimes it is a drawn out *b-e-e-e-b.*

2. A **horn** is often a combination of a high and a low tone. It sounds a throaty blast like some automobile horns.

3. A **siren** has a varying tone which rises and falls, like the sirens still used on some police cars, ambulances, and fire engines.

Buoy-to-Buoy Navigation

At times of fog or when visibility is restricted during a storm, it is often better to chart courses from buoy to buoy in order to have check points, rather than choosing a shorter and more direct route to a destination. The navigator should note especially the types of audible aids along the track and should be able to describe the sound characteristic of a buoy or structure whenever he asks the crew to listen for it. Note the following examples.

1. A **bell** makes one tone. Usually four clappers are attached to the rim of the structure, and they hit a single large bell suspended from the center.
2. A **gong** usually has four heavy-metal squashed bells, one under another in graduated sizes. Hanging from the top of the structure on metal rods of graduated lengths are four clappers, and each one strikes only one bell. The bells are struck at random, so that all four tones may or may not be heard.
3. A **whistle** makes a single-toned *maw-w-w*, like a hoarse cow, or else a higher-pitched *eu-u-u*.

The *Light List* has this to say about sound buoys: "Fog signals on buoys are generally actuated by the motion of the sea and, therefore, do not emit regular signal characteristics, and when the sea is calm, may emit no sound signals."

Sheltered Side of Islands

As the wind blows across an island, the warmer air rising from the land tends to evaporate the fog temporarily, and less fog or no fog at all is likely to be close to the island shoreline which is sheltered from the wind. Thus, an attempt should be made to chart a course to take advantage of this possibility.

The two places where this is particularly sensible are Maine and south of Cape Cod. We have often charted courses in Maine from the sheltered side of one island to another, after we first checked the chart carefully to make sure there was deep water up to the shoreline of the next island along the way. South of Cape Cod, the fog very often will be thick on the Vineyard Sound side of the Elizabeth Islands, yet there will be a path of remarkably good visibility along the shores of these islands on the Buzzard's Bay side.

Instrument Navigation

The primary rule in fog is to believe the information derived from the navigational instruments aboard. As fog can move in quickly along a coast, skippers should be ready for it whenever they leave the harbor. Instruments, such as the compass, RDF, and so forth, should have fixed locations where either there is no deviation or the amount of deviation is known.

The lonely feeling of being surrounded by a fog bank can cause momentary panic. We know of one couple, cruising off the coast of California, who motored around in circles for a while after the fog set in in order to determine what to do. They turned on the RDF and followed the reciprocal of the bearing for some distance into the Pacific Ocean before they discovered their mistake. They did not know how to check the direction of the radiobeacon. (An explanation of how to do this is given in chapter 22.)

When homing on a navigational aid in a fog by means of an RDF bearing, it is advisable not only to keep track of the time and distance covered, but also to maintain a bow watch when nearing the aid in order to have a little sea room at the proper moment. This should also be done when following compass courses. There are many stories of persons who navigated so accurately in a fog that they actually ran into a navigational aid.

22

Night Cruising

In areas where there are lighted navigational aids, cruising after dark in clear weather can be a very pleasant experience when the chart has been studied carefully ahead of time. Even though the landmarks frequently used in daylight cruising are no longer visible, the lighted aids serve as long-distance guideposts along a coast, and lighted ranges clearly mark the channels into many harbors. The light characteristics of the various lighted aids can be found in the *Light List*.

The lights required to be shown aboard boats from sunset to sunrise are called **running lights** and clearly identify whether a boat is under power or sail, as well as the direction in which the boat is moving. The arrangement of additional lights, other than the navigational lights required for all boats, indicates the various kinds of activity, usually commercial, in which boats are engaged.

All the lights required by the U.S. Coast Guard to be shown aboard boats from sunset to sunrise are described fully in the three pamphlets published by this service: *Rules of the Road: International-Inland*; *Rules of the Road: Great Lakes*; and *Rules of the Road: Western Rivers* (see appendix I). The most recent edition of the pamphlet for your cruising area should be read carefully and kept aboard for reference.

The required horizontal arc of each light is described in degrees and points in the *Rules of the Road* and is usually referred to in poin̂ts by boatmen. **Points** are derived from a mariner's compass card, on which the principal, or cardinal, points of the compass, 'N' (north), 'E' (east), 'S' (south), and 'W' (west), are subdivided eight times. Each point, such as N to N by E, equals $11\frac{1}{4}°$; 32 points equal 360°.

The term **abeam,** which is mentioned frequently in the *Rules of the Road,* is considered to be 90° to the center line of the boat at its widest part.

The International Rules concerning lights not only apply on the high seas but may also be used on inland waters as well (unless otherwise specified). The navigational requirements for boats under 65 feet in length, as set forth in rule 7 and rule 10, are listed below for quick reference. The light requirements of the Inland Rules for dinghies under power, sail, or propelled by oars are also included. The Inland Rules apply close to shore along the coasts and in harbors as well as on many lakes and rivers. The boundary lines for inland waters are described in the *Rules of the Road.*

Yacht Navigational or Running Lights
(*Rules of the Road*)

Some of the Rules for lights on boats follow.

Power-driven boats of less than 65 feet:
A 20-point (225°) unbroken white light showing forward and 10 points on each side, or from the bow to 2 points abaft the beam; should be visible at a distance of at least 3 miles. This light is carried at least 9 feet higher than the colored side lights.
A 12-point (135°) unbroken white stern light (Interna-

tional Rule), positioned at the center line of the boat, should show aft from 2 points abaft the beam on each side and should be visible at a distance of at least 2 miles. Although the height of the stern light is not specified in the International Rules, the Inland Rules require that it be positioned at approximately the level of the side lights.

A 10-point (112½°) red light is required on the port side and a 10-point green light on the starboard side. Each side light must not show across the bow and must be visible at least 1 mile. International Rules also state that a red-and-green lantern may be carried forward in place of the side lights. It also must be visible for 1 mile and must be carried not less than 3 feet below the 20-point white light.

Auxiliary sailboats under power:

The light requirements for power-driven boats apply.

Auxiliary sailboats under sail alone, or sailboats under sail:

These boats use the same red-and-green side lights and the 12-point stern light required for power-driven boats, but do not use the 20-point bow light.

Power-driven boats of less than 26 feet in inland waters:

These boats carry a combination red-and-green lantern forward and a 32-point (360°) all-around white stern light visible for a distance of at least 2 miles. This stern light may be off the center line of the boat when the position of an outboard motor makes it impossible to do otherwise.

Dinghies (rowboats) under sail or propelled by oars:

A powerful flashlight or lantern is carried, and the white light is shown in time to prevent a collision. The flashlight beam should be shone on the sail from time to time, to identify your craft.

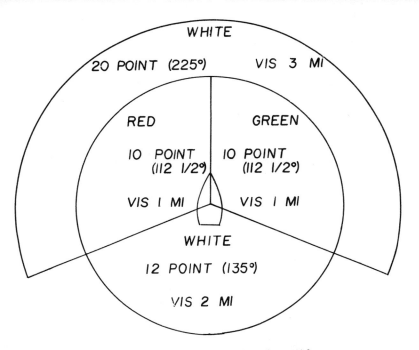

Fig. 26. Lights for power-driven boats of less than 65 feet.

(Includes auxiliaries under power or under sail and power.)

Fig. 27. Lights for sailboats under sail.

(Includes auxiliaries under sail alone.)

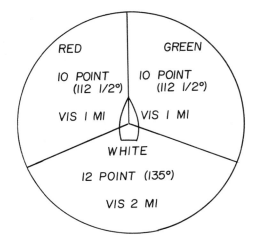

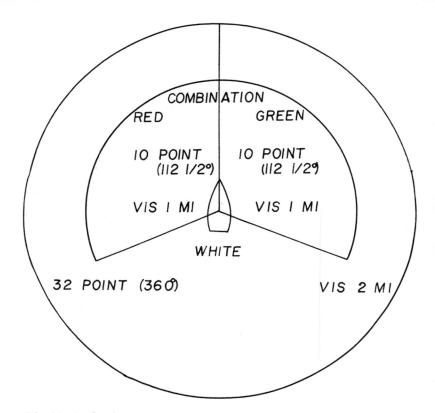

Fig. 28. Lights for power-driven boats of less than 26 feet.

Memory Aids for Lights

Memory aids for the proper sides for the colored side lights are: "Port is the color of red, red wine," and "each word in the grouping 'port, left, red' has fewer letters than each word in the grouping 'starboard, right, green'."

There is also a poem to help you remember what to do when a boat is coming toward you on a collision course: you give one blast with the horn and alter course to starboard in order to pass port to port.

When both lights you see ahead,
Turn to starboard and show your red,
For green to green or red to red
Is perfectly safe to go ahead.

Visibility of Lighted Navigational Aids

The distance from a lighted navigational aid and certain weather conditions influence the ability of an observer to recognize the specific characteristics of light combinations. Under all weather conditions white lights are visible at a greater distance than colored lights. Haze and other conditions of lessened visibility tend to further shorten the distance at which colored lights can be seen. A combination light that has a characteristic of alternating colors, such as white with either red or green, at first sighting will usually appear to be white alone.

At night one of the most confusing things is spotting lighted aids along a shoreline ablaze with the lights of towns and cities, and even the headlights of cars on busy highways. Flashing neon lights and blinking red traffic lights vie with the flashing lights on navigational aids. We once had the annoying experience of finally locating what we thought to be a fixed red light on a navigational aid, only to have it turn green.

The best way we have found to identify a lighted aid against this type of background is to keep an eye on a particular light as the boat is moving along the coastline. The light on a navigational aid will actually seem to be moving in the opposite direction along the shoreline in relation to fixed objects ashore, while lights on the shore will stay in place.

Reflectors

Many buoys are outfitted with reflectors, which are usually red on red buoys, and green or white on black buoys. The color of a reflector on a specific buoy can be found in the *Light List*. By moving the beam of a powerful searchlight back and forth along the horizon in the direction of a buoy, it is possible to sight the reflector before the buoy itself is seen.

Entering a Harbor After Dark

When entering a harbor at night, we station a lookout on the bow with a searchlight. He is instructed to call out the colors of buoy reflectors as he picks them up with the light, and to report the numbers of the buoys as they become visible. The lookout is also cautioned to keep the searchlight beam on the nearest buoy until the skipper can clear it readily. The searchlight in the hands of a nervous horizon-sweeper offers little help to the skipper.

The lookout locates obstructions such as boats, moorings, anchor lines, piers, and lobster pots with the light. Once again, he keeps the searchlight beam on the object until he is sure the skipper will clear the obstruction.

A searchlight must be handled with care so the skippers of other boats, or even persons aboard your own boat, are not blinded by the powerful beam. If the beam is always directed low when you wish to identify a boat, the night vision of the other crew will not be disturbed. Flashing a light into the pilothouse of another boat is illegal, as specifically set forth in the *Rules of the Road.*

Lighting Aboard When Under Way

When cruising at night, it is important that the skipper is shielded from any white lights aboard so that his night vision will not be impaired. Red instrument-panel and compass lights will help you maintain night vision. This can be accomplished by buying red bulbs, if you can find them, or by painting bulbs with either the red lacquer sold for this purpose or red nail polish, which seems to do the job as well. Painting the bulbs of one or two flashlights will be helpful to the skipper who may wish to check the charts himself from time to time.

Pitfalls

When cruising on a clear night, there is a tendency to become so entranced with the arching, star-spattered sky and the flecks of wave-tossed phosphorus glittering in the wake, that you may not be as alert to the pitfalls of night cruising as you should be. Having a buoy loom suddenly out of the night, when you have been swept along by the current faster than anticipated, makes you realize the need to keep an alert deck watch before you expect to near a buoy.

In places where there are fish traps, like the Chesapeake Bay, it is wise to give wide berth to the areas where these are charted, because a propeller can easily be fouled in these nets. The nets are supposed to be lighted, but they are still hard to spot.

To keep one hand for yourself and one for the boat is even more essential at night. Even when the sea is calm, it is difficult to observe the wash from boats in the area. A large freighter passing in the distance is beautiful to see with its bright lights, but a large wave can come along soon after to toss your boat about and drench unwary passengers.

One of the greater pitfalls to be encountered in night cruising is the possibility of hitting something floating in the water. This is especially likely to happen after a severe storm in the area; nearly submerged pieces of docks, trees, and sometimes even telephone poles may then be floating around. In this case, as well as at the entrance to a large harbor, it is advisable to have someone on the bow with a powerful flashlight to look for flotsam and jetsam.

It is possible to become confused when cruising at night. We know of one skipper who became confused and could not find the approach into an unfamiliar harbor. He turned on his depth sounder and slowly made his way toward land until the water was shoal enough for him to anchor. He put up his anchor light and enjoyed a good sleep in his rocking berth until dawn.

Appendix I

Publications

WE BELIEVE that all yachtsmen should be familiar with the following publications, and most of them should be kept aboard a cruising boat. For your convenience we list here all the publications we mention in the text of this book. This list can be used at fitting-out time to ensure that you have aboard all the references you might need.

Those publications issued by the National Ocean Survey of the National Oceanic and Atmospheric Administration (NOAA) can be purchased from authorized nautical chart agents or ordered directly. Most of the other publications are available in marine supply stores or can be ordered by them. Naturally, the prices listed are subject to change.

AUTHORIZED NAUTICAL CHART AGENTS. Order
    pamphlet from:
    U.S. Department of Commerce
    NOAA
    National Ocean Survey
    Rockville, Maryland 20852   free
    (The Lake Survey Center lists the official chart sales

agents for the Great Lakes in its NAUTICAL CHART CATALOG.)

CHARTS. May be purchased from authorized chart agents. The area covered by each chart is superimposed on a map of the coastline in NAUTICAL CHART CATALOGS, and charts are listed with their prices. Order from:

Distribution Division (C44)
National Ocean Survey
Riverdale, Maryland 20840

COAST PILOTS. A series of eight books containing information important to navigators of United States coastal and intracoastal waters. These books may be obtained from an authorized chart agent or ordered from:

U.S. Department of Commerce
NOAA
National Ocean Survey
Rockville, Maryland 20852 $2.00

(Great Lakes) MONTHLY BULLETIN OF LAKE LEVELS. Order from:

U.S. Department of Commerce
NOAA
Lake Survey Center
630 Federal Building
Detroit, Michigan 48226   free

GREAT LAKES PILOT (including supplements). Order from:

U.S. Department of Commerce
NOAA
Lake Survey Center
630 Federal Building
Detroit, Michigan 48226 $5.25

LIGHT LIST. Published in four volumes, which may be obtained from an authorized chart agent or from:

Superintendent of Documents
U.S. Government Printing Office
Washington, D.C. 20402 $7.75
For Great Lakes LIGHT LIST, *order from:*
U.S. Coast Guard Cleveland District Office
Coast Guard Base
Sault Ste. Marie, Michigan 49783 $7.75
MARINE WEATHER SERVICES CHARTS. Order
from:
Superintendent of Documents
U.S. Government Printing Office
Washington, D.C. 20402 $.25
NAUTICAL CHART CATALOGS. Order from:
U.S. Department of Commerce
NOAA
National Ocean Survey
Rockville, Maryland 20852   free
For Great Lakes NAUTICAL CHART CATALOGS,
order from:
U.S. Department of Commerce
NOAA
Lake Survey Center
630 Federal Building
Detroit, Michigan 48226   free
or from:
Canadian Hydrographic Service
Marine Sciences Branch
Department of Mines and Technical Surveys
Ottawa, Canada   free
NAUTICAL CHART SYMBOLS AND ABBREVIA-
TIONS (CHART #1). Order from:
U.S. Department of Commerce
NOAA
National Ocean Survey
Rockville, Maryland 20852 $.50

or from:
Lake Survey Center
630 Federal Building
Detroit, Michigan 48226 $.50
NOTICE TO MARINERS. Published weekly by the U.S. Naval Oceanographic Office, in two parts: part I, "Atlantic Ocean and Mediterranean Sea"; part II, "Pacific and Indian Oceans." Order from:
U.S. Department of Commerce
NOAA
National Ocean Survey
Rockville, Maryland 20852   free
Of more use, however, to the cruising yachtsman is the local NOTICE TO MARINERS *issued by each U.S. Coast Guard district. You can receive this free of charge by either writing or calling the office of the U.S. Coast Guard district commander in your area to request that your name be placed on the mailing list. Call your local Coast Guard station to find the address of the district office. Coast Guard stations are listed in the telephone book under:*
United States Government
Transportation Department
Coast Guard
RULES OF THE ROAD: International—Inland (CG-169)
RULES OF THE ROAD: Great Lakes (CG-172)
RULES OF THE ROAD: Western Rivers (CG-184)
You may obtain copies from U.S. Coast Guard marine inspection offices in major ports, from some authorized chart agents, or by writing to:
Commandant (GCAS)
U.S. Coast Guard
400 7th Street, S.W.
Washington, D.C. 20590   free

SECTIONAL AERONAUTICAL CHARTS. May be purchased at local airports or ordered from:
U.S. Department of Commerce
NOAA
National Ocean Survey
Rockville, Maryland 20852 $1.19

TIDAL CURRENT CHARTS. A set of twelve charts. These are listed, with their prices, in the NAUTICAL CHART CATALOGS. The charts may be purchased from an authorized chart agent or ordered from:
U.S. Department of Commerce
NOAA
National Ocean Survey
Rockville, Maryland 20852

TIDAL CURRENT TABLES. Published in two volumes: "Atlantic Coast of North America" and "Pacific Coast of North America." These may be purchased from an authorized chart agent or ordered from:
U.S. Department of Commerce
NOAA
National Ocean Survey
Rockville, Maryland 20852 $2.00

TIDE TABLES: High and Low Water Predictions. May be purchased from an authorized chart agent or ordered from:
U.S. Department of Commerce
NOAA
National Ocean Survey
Rockville, Maryland 20852 $2.00

Appendix II

Quick-Reference Lists

THIS SECTION IS INTENDED as a quick reference while you are navigating aboard your boat, in order to help you refresh your memory in a hurry. Only the situations you are likely to encounter most frequently are included. For complete coverage, refer to the text of the book and to the reference material listed in appendix I.

For your convenience we are including some of the **right of way** rules as defined by the *Rules of the Road*, and also some **distress signals**.

LIST A
CHART LANGUAGE

The government publication *Nautical Chart Symbols and Abbreviations (Chart #1)* translates almost 1,000 entries. The following is a listing of some of the most common chart markings and their explanations.

General

When entering a harbor:
  - a) red aids are kept to starboard (right) of the helmsman ("red–right–returning from the sea").
  - b) black aids are kept to port (left) of the helmsman. (When leaving a harbor: black to starboard, red to port.)

A dot (.) indicates the location of a navigational aid. It is found:
  - a) adjacent to a diamond buoy symbol.
  - b) in the center of a solid-red circle symbol of a lighted aid.
  - c) adjacent to a solid-red teardrop symbol of a lighted aid.

Buoys

(Further description of the structures may be found in the *Light List*.)

◻   Anchored marker

Solid-red diamond   Any red-painted buoy
   N   Nun—red solid structure,
                          conical

BELL, GONG, or WHISTLE	Red sound buoy—usually a skeleton structure
Solid-black diamond C	Any black-painted buoy Can—black solid structure, cylindrical, flat-topped
BELL, GONG, or WHISTLE	Black sound buoy—usually a skeleton structure
Half red, half black diamond	Red-and-black horizontally banded solid or skeleton structure, marking a midchannel fork or obstruction; top band denotes preferred channel (Example: if top band is red, preferred channel is to keep buoy to starboard when returning from the sea)
RB	Red/black
Diamond outline with vertical line through it	Black-and-white vertically striped solid or skeleton structure, marking midchannel of a fairway; pass on either side
BW	Black/white

Daybeacons

(Further description of the structures may be found in the *Light List*.)

Δ   Fixed marker (location in center of triangle)

Bn	Beacon
Red triangle	Red-painted marker
Black triangle	Black-painted marker
Triangle outline	Marker of unknown color

Range Structures

(Description of the structures may be found in the *Light List*.)

⊙----⊙--- ——————— Aligned structures; a range is followed only for the distance of solid line (when not lighted, range structures are symbolized by day-beacon triangles)

Radiobeacons

(Further information concerning transmission may be found in the "General Information" section of the *Light List*.)

 Station transmitting RDF (radio direction finder) signal

R Bn	Radiobeacon
Number (3 digits)	Frequency of beacon
Dot-dash combination	Sound characteristic of signal
DFS	Distance finding station; sends a special signal to enable determination of approximate distance of boat from station

Lighted Aids

(Further description of the characteristics of lights is given in the *Light List*.)

⊙ (red) or ♪(red)	Lighthouse structure; lighted range structure; lighted beacon; or, when accompanying a diamond symbol, lighted buoy
W	White light
R	Red light
G	Green light (if on a buoy, assume buoy is black)
E Int	Equal intervals of lighted and eclipsed (dark) periods
F	Fixed (steady) light
Fl	Flashing—short lighted periods
Occ	Occulting—short eclipsed periods
Qk Fl	Quick-flashing
I Qk Fl	Interrupted quick-flashing
S–L	Short–long flashes
Mo (A)	Morse code *A* (dot–dash) short–long flashes
Alt	Alternating (color change)
Gp	Group sequence, with eclipsed period between groups
Sec	Seconds

Landmarks

TR	Tower
R TR	Radio tower

CUP	Cupola or dome on roof
STACK	Smokestack
S'PIPE	Standpipe or water tower

Water Depth

Buff area	Land
Blue area	Water to from 1 to 6 fathoms deep—limit varies with chart (1 fathom = 6 feet)
White area	Water deeper than blue area
+ or ✳ (surrounded by dotted line)	Rocks
or	Riprap (rockpile) around a lighted beacon
Numbers printed in blue or white area	Soundings; chart heading will state water level on which soundings are based and whether they are in feet, fathoms, or feet/fathoms (Example of feet/fathoms: 4_2 = 4 fathoms 2 feet)
Dotted, dashed, or solid black line (like a map contour line)	Fathom line; dots and dashes coded in *Chart #1*

Bottom Characteristics

S	Sand
M	Mud
Rk	Rocks
rky	Rocky
K	Kelp
Wd	Seaweed
grs	Grass

Compass Rose

Double circle of numbers, about 4″ in diameter	000° to 360°, to be used for course and bearing directions; positioning mark ('+') in center must be intersected with parallel-ruler edge or the like (a line extended through both circles shows both true and magnetic degrees of that line)
Outer circle, star at 0°	True-degrees circle—star at true (geographic) north
Inner circle, arrow at 0°	Magnetic-degrees circle—arrow at magnetic north; used with magnetic compass
VAR	Variation figure (printed in center); difference in degrees between true and magnetic north for that particular area

Latitude and Longitude

Lines parallel to equator numbered from 0°N to 90°N and from 0°S to 90°S	Parallels of latitude written in degrees, minutes, and tenths of minutes—as: Lat. 0°01.1′N); 'N' = north of equator, 'S' = south of equator (U.S.A. latitude always 'N')

Margin scales at sides of chart	Latitude scales; used to measure both latitude and nautical mileage (60′ = 1°); 1 minute (′) of latitude = 1 nautical mile, 1 degree (°) of latitude = 60 nautical miles
Lines perpendicular to equator numbered from 0°W to 180°W and from 0°E to 180°E	Meridians of longitude (written in degrees, minutes, and tenths of minutes—as: Long. 0°01.1′W); 'W' = west of prime meridian at Greenwich, England (0°), 'E' = east of prime meridian (U.S.A. longitude always 'W')
Margin scales at top and bottom of chart	Longitude scales; used to measure longitude only (60′ = 1°)

LIST B
PLOTTING PROCEDURES

The following common examples of plotting, as well as others used less frequently, are covered in detail in the text of this book; they can be found by consulting the index.

General

The four cardinal points (principal directions) of a compass and their equivalent degree readings:
   a) North = 000° or 360°.
   b) East = 090°.
   c) South = 180°.
   d) West = 270°.
Use of degrees on chart compass roses and your ship's compass ("*True Virgins Make Dull Companions*"):
   True degrees—compass rose outer circle.
   Variation (earth's magnetism at location of compass rose)—difference between true and magnetic degree readings.
   Magnetic degrees—compass rose inner circle.
   Deviation (magnetic influences on your boat)—difference between magnetic and compass degree readings.
   Compass—Your ship's compass reading.
   a) "From true add west" for variation and deviation.
   b) Work down the steps to determine steering degrees for your ship's compass.
   c) Work up the steps to plot a bearing on a chart.
Distance/speed/time formula:
   a) Distance (*D*) is measured in nautical miles (statute miles used on the Great Lakes, the Mississippi River, and intracoastal waterways).

b) Speed (S) is measured in knots (miles per hour used when distance is measured in statute miles).

c) Time (T) is figured in minutes.

$$D = \frac{S \times T}{60} \qquad S = \frac{D \times 60}{T} \qquad T = \frac{D \times 60}{S}$$

24-hour time:

a) Midnight = 24^h00^m of old day or 00^h00^m of new day.

b) Noon = 12^h00^m ("after noon, add 12").

c) Used in ship's log book, for plotting ETA (estimated time of arrival), time of sighting LOPs (lines of position), and boat's probable position on DR (dead reckoning) track.

Course Line

1. *Buoy-to-buoy:*

C 102°MAG   6.2 MI   C 282°MAG

1032   S 6   ETA 1134

Translation:

a) First buoy passed close aboard at 10^h32^m.

b) Course to next buoy is 102° magnetic (inner circle of compass rose).

c) Distance between buoys is 6.2 nautical miles.

d) At a boat speed of 6 knots, estimated time of arrival at second buoy is 11^h34^m.

e) Reciprocal (return) course is 282° magnetic.

2. *DR (dead reckoning) track:*

1200 DR

C 102°MAG

S 8

Translation: On course 102° magnetic with a boat speed of 8 knots, the probable position of the boat at 12ʰ00ᵐ is marked and circled on the course line. A DR track should be kept during fog and heavy rainstorms or for any considerable amount of time that the boat is out of sight of land and navigational aids. The position is marked and the time recorded:

a) every whole hour.

b) whenever course direction is changed.

c) whenever speed is changed.

d) when a single line of position is established.

Note: A new track to the destination is started whenever a fix or a running fix is established and it does not correspond with the DR position.

Single Line of Position

(The boat is located somewhere along this line.)

1. Range:

$$\frac{1253}{\text{RANGE}}$$

(Line is drawn through range location dots to the course line.)

Translation: At 12ʰ53ᵐ range is aligned from boat.

2. Navigational aid abeam:

$$\frac{1103}{\text{ABEAM}}$$

(Line is drawn perpendicular to the course line and the boat must be on the charted course degrees at the time of sighting.)

Translation: At 11ʰ03ᵐ the aid is sighted so that the line of sight forms a right angle with the center line of the boat, and the boat is heading on the charted course.

3. Visual bearing on navigational aid:

$$\frac{1526}{102°\,\text{MAG}}$$

(Line is drawn from the aid to the course line using the reciprocal (opposite) direction of the bearing; then line is labeled with the number of degrees of bearing from the boat.)

Translation: At 15ʰ36ᵐ the aid is 102° magnetic from the boat.

Note: If there is deviation in the compass, be sure to use the deviation for the degree reading of the boat's heading, *not* of the bearing of the aid, in order to determine the number of magnetic degrees of the bearing.

Pelorus: When the number of degrees of the bearing is determined from a fixed azimuth card (aligned with the 000°–180° axis parallel to the center line of the boat), it is a relative bearing; this number is then added to the reading of the ship's compass heading at the exact moment of sighting. (If there is deviation, it must be applied to the ship's compass heading to make it a magnetic heading.)

Fix

Two or more bearings taken on different navigational aids within 1 minute establish the position of the boat. Preferably these bearings should be 90° apart.

1. Visual bearings:

$$\frac{1030}{268°\,\text{MAG}} \qquad \frac{1030}{163°\,\text{MAG}}$$

Translation: At 10ʰ30ᵐ (or within 1 minute of this time) two bearings are sighted: one 268° magnetic from the boat and the other 163° magnetic.

2. Fix:

⊙ 1030 FIX

(A circle is drawn around the intersection of two or more bearing lines or at a dot placed in the center of a triangle formed by three lines.)

Translation: At 10ʰ30ᵐ the position of the boat is established at this point on the chart. (When bearings have been taken with an electronic device, its name is included in the labeling, as: 'RAD FIX', for "radar"; 'LORAN FIX', for "loran"; 'OMEGA FIX', for "Omega"; 'OMNI FIX', for "omnirange.")

Note: A new course line to the destination is started whenever a fix does not correspond with the previous course line.

Running Fix

Usually two bearings are taken at different times on the same navigational aid.

1. First and second visual bearings:

$$\frac{1250}{075°\text{MAG}} \qquad \frac{1320}{003°\text{MAG}}$$

Translation: At 12ʰ50ᵐ an aid is 075° magnetic from the boat; half an hour later, at 13ʰ20ᵐ, the aid is 003° from the boat.

2. Advanced first bearing:

$$\frac{1250-1320}{075°\text{MAG}}$$

Translation: After the distance traveled along the course in the 30 minutes between the sightings is determined by $D = (S \times T) \div 60$, and marked on the course line, parallel rulers are placed on the 1250 bearing line, and this line is then transposed to the mark and drawn.

3. *Running fix:*

⊙ 1250–1320 R Fix

(A circle is drawn around the intersection of the second bearing line and advanced first bearing line.)

Translation: At 13^{h}20^m the position of the boat is established at this point on the chart.

Note: A new course line to the destination is started whenever a running fix does not correspond with the previous course line.

Radio Direction Finder Estimated Position

Two or more bearings taken on different radiobeacons as close to the same time as possible establish an estimated position (EP) of the boat. (Since radio bearings are less accurate than visual or other electronic bearings, a new course line is not started toward the destination if the EP does not correspond with the course line.)

1. *Radio bearings:*

1030	1030
022°MAG	126°MAG

Translation: As near to 10^{h}30^m as possible one radiobeacon is determined to be 022° magnetic from the boat, and another 126° magnetic.

2. Estimated position:

■ 1030 EP

(A square is drawn around the intersection of the two bearing lines.)

Translation: At 10^h30^m the estimated position of the boat is at this point on the chart.

Note: If the EP is not on the course line, alter course if there is possible danger ahead, recheck the bearings using other radiobeacons if possible, and get visual bearings at the first opportunity.

LIST C
NAUTICAL AND STATUTE
MILEAGE EQUIVALENTS

A statute mile is 5,280 feet in length; a nautical mile is 1.15 statute miles, or 6,076 feet. In this table we have rounded off the statute miles to tenths (for example: 1 nautical mile = 1.2 statute miles).

Miles		Miles	
Nautical (knots)	Statute (mph)	Nautical (knots)	Statute (mph)
1	1.2	16	18.4
2	2.3	17	19.6
3	3.5	18	20.7
4	4.6	19	21.9
5	5.8	20	23.0
6	6.9	21	24.2
7	8.1	22	25.3
8	9.2	23	26.5
9	10.4	24	27.6
10	11.5	25	28.8
11	12.7	26	29.9
12	13.8	27	31.1
13	15.0	28	32.2
14	16.1	29	33.4
15	17.3	30	34.5

LIST D
LIGHTS CARRIED ON BOATS
UNDER WAY

The many and varied light arrangements and visibilities required for different types of boats in different waters are described in the federal government publications *Rules of the Road*. There are three of these, published for three different areas:

    a) *International-Inland.* This book lists two separate sets of rules. It also defines and describes the specific boundary lines between waters offshore (international) and waters along and in from the United States coastline. Briefly, "the waters inshore of a line approximately parallel with the general trend of the shore, drawn through the outermost buoy or other aid to navigation or any system of aids, are inland waters. . . ."

    b) *Great Lakes.*

    c) *Western Rivers.*

We suggest you consult whichever *Rules of the Road* volume covers your boating waters. A selection from the Inland Rules is given here for quick reference. (Where the International or Great Lakes Rules are not the same as the Inland Rule, the difference is noted.) Also see chapter 22 of this book for a detailed discussion of light requirements.

Lights are required to be shown from sunset to sunrise on all waters. Powerboats and sailboats under 65 feet are required to show the following lights.

    a) Stern light: A bright white light aft to show all around the horizon—32-point, or 360°. (International Rules: 12-point, or 135°, white light.)

b) Side lights: A 10-point, or $112\frac{1}{2}°$, red light to port; a 10-point, or $112\frac{1}{2}°$, green light to starboard. Boats under International Rules may carry either separate side lights or a combination red-and-green lantern on the bow, positioned lower than the white stern light; the lantern must show red to port and green to starboard. (Side lights or combination lantern lights are prevented from being seen across the bow.) Memory aid: "Port," "left," and "red" have fewer letters than "starboard," "right," and "green."

c) Bow light: A 20-point, or $225°$, white light for a power-driven vessel, including an auxiliary sailboat under power. (This light is not used by vessels under sail alone.)

LIST E
FOG SIGNALS GIVEN BY BOATS

These and other rules are discussed in detail in *Rules of the Road*, described in quick-reference list D. (Where the International or Great Lakes Rules are not the same as the Inland Rules, the difference is noted.)

Power Boats Under Way

1 prolonged blast (4 to 6 seconds) at least every minute. (International: 1 prolonged blast (4 to 6 seconds) at least every 2 minutes. Great Lakes: 3 distinct blasts at least every minute.)

Sailboats Under Way

Short blasts at least every minute:
  a) Starboard tack: 1 blast.
  b) Port tack: 2 blasts.
  c) Wind abaft the beam: 3 blasts.

Vessels at Anchor in a Fairway

A bell rung rapidly for about 5 seconds at least every minute. (Great Lakes: A bell rung rapidly for 3 to 5 seconds at least every 2 minutes; in addition, a signal of 1 short blast, 2 long blasts, and 1 short blast in quick succession at intervals of not more than 3 minutes.)

LIST F
FOG SIGNALS FROM
NAVIGATIONAL AIDS

Sound buoys that are operated by the action of the sea will not be heard in a flat calm. For the duration and frequency of each lighthouse sound signal, consult the *Light List.*

Bell (buoy)	1 tone
Gong (buoy)	4 tones (all 4 tones may not be heard, but at least 2 will be distinguished)
Whistle (buoy)	Either low in pitch (*maw-w-w*) or higher (*eu-u-u*)
Diaphone (lighthouse)	*Bee-bah* or *be-e-e-eb*
Horn (lighthouse)	Similar to an automobile horn
Siren (lighthouse)	Varying pitch—similar to an ambulance or police car

LIST G
RIGHT-OF-WAY

These and other rules appear in *Rules of the Road*, described in quick-reference list D. (Where the Great Lakes Rules are not the same as the Inland Rules, the difference is noted.)

The burdened boat is responsible for taking action; the privileged boat is responsible for maintaining a steady course and speed. However, the privileged boat must take action when necessary to avoid collision with the burdened boat.

Boats Under Power
(Including Auxiliary Sailboats)

Right-of-way.
- a) Head-on meeting: Both boats are burdened; each shall alter course to starboard so as to pass port to port. (See "Whistle signals" below.)
- b) Crossing situation: Burdened boat is the one that has the other on her starboard side.
- c) Overtaking situation: Burdened boat is the overtaking one.
- d) Meeting with a sailboat: Powerboat is burdened in all cases except when the sailboat is the overtaking boat.

Whistle signals. The whistle signal is a signal of action. In inland and Great Lakes waters, all signals except the inland backing signal must be answered with a like signal before action is taken.
- a) Danger signal: 5 or more short, rapid blasts. (Great Lakes: Several short, rapid blasts.) This signal is used

to indicate that you do not understand the signal of another boat or that you do not believe sufficient action is being taken by the other boat to avoid collision.

b) Approaching situation: 1 short blast—boats can pass safely port to port or should alter course to do so; 2 short blasts—boats can pass safely starboard to starboard.

c) Overtaking situation: 1 short blast—burdened boat wishes to pass to starboard of boat ahead; 2 short blasts—boat wishes to pass to port of boat ahead.

d) Visibility obstructed by a curve, in a narrow channel, or when leaving a dock: 1 long blast. (Great Lakes: At least an 8-second signal.)

e) Backing signal: 3 short blasts. (Great Lakes: No specific backing signal; 3 short blasts used instead as a fog signal for powerboats under way.)

Drawbridge opening signals. The usual signal is 3 distinct blasts. (This is not a Rule of the Road; further bridge information can be found in the "Navigation Regulations" as well as the text for the particular area in the appropriate volume of the *Coast Pilot.*)

Sailboats Under Sail Alone

Right-of-way.

a) Two boats approaching each other on different tacks: Port tack boat (wind over the port side) is burdened when meeting a starboard tack boat.

b) Two boats on same tack heading in same direction: Windward (upwind) boat is burdened.

c) Two boats on same tack heading in different directions: Boat running free (wind abaft her beam) is burdened when meeting a boat more closely hauled (sailing closer to the wind).

Signals. No specific signals are required, but courtesy and safety dictate that the privileged boat call the burdened boat's attention to the conditions. Example: A boat on the starboard tack calls "Starboard!" to the boat on the port tack and holds course, unless the burdened boat takes no action and appears to be in danger of collision. At this moment, the privileged boat alters course to avoid collision.

LIST H
DISTRESS SIGNALS

a) Slowly and repeatedly raising and lowering arms outstretched to each side.

b) Continuous sounding of fog signaling device.

c) S–O–S (. . . _ _ _ . . .) signaled with mirror or flashlight.

d) Flares (including smoke).

e) International Code signal flags of distress: N–C.

f) Surface-to-air distress flag: 72- by 45-inch orange-red flag with 18-inch black circle and 18-inch black square across it.

g) Radiotelephone: "Mayday, Mayday, Mayday" said on distress channel 7 (156.3), distress frequency SSB 2182, or any frequency.

h) National flag flown upside down.

i) Fire or smoke from a bucket on deck.

j) Specially designed distress flags as authorized for this purpose by state authorities.

Index

(For illustrations see list in front of book.)

Abeam, 179
  navigational aids, 92 (quick
    reference, 202)
Aeronautical signals, RDF, 141
Alternating light, 23, 183
Anchoring in a fairway, fog
    signal for, 172
Approaching whistle signal
    (quick reference), 213
Authorized Chart Agents, 35
    (to obtain, 187)
Automatic RDF, 142
Auxiliary sailboat, *see* Power-
    boat; Sailboat
Azimuth card, 89–90
  RDF, 131

Backing whistle signal (quick
    reference), 213
Bamboo pole for depth, 130
Beacon, 12–13
    (*See also* Daybeacon; Radio-
    beacon)
Bearing, 85–95 (quick refer-
    ence, 203, 204, 205)
  danger, 96–98
  relative, 89–92
  "True Virgins Conversion
    Steps" for, 44–46, 86–88
Beating, 117–119
Bell buoy, 13, 14, 175 (quick
    reference, 194, 211)
Binoculars, 72–73, 173

Black (used for navigational
    aids), 14–16 (quick refer-
    ence, 194)
Boat speed, 60–61
Bottom characteristics (quick
    reference), 197
    depth sounder and, 126
Bow, 5
    and running lights, 179–180
Bow and beam bearing, 93–95
Bow watch, *see* Lookout
Bridge, opening signals for
    (quick reference), 213
    heights of, 26, 167–168
Buoy, 4–6, 12–16, 175 (quick
    reference, 193–194, 211)
    reflectors on, 184
    (*See also* Lights on naviga-
    tional aids; Navigational
    aids)
Burdened boat (quick refer-
    ence), 212–214

Can buoy, 14 (quick reference,
    193)
Center line, 41–42
Channel, 15, 24, 82, 128–129
Chart agents, 35
Charting, *see* Plotting
Charts:
    for loran use, 147
    *Marine Weather Services
    Charts* (to purchase),
    189
    nautical, 3–38 (to purchase,
    188; quick reference, 193–
    199)

Nautical Chart Catalogs, 38–
    39 (to purchase, 189)
*Nautical Chart Symbols and
    Abbreviations (Chart #1),*
    12 (to purchase, 189)
    for omni station location,
    153
    for RDF use, 141–142
Sectional Aeronautical Charts
    (to purchase), 191
Tidal Current Charts, 156–
    157 (to purchase, 191)
Chart table, 69
"Church steeple" navigation,
    40, 170
Circle of distance, 105–110
Coast charts, 36
Coast Pilots, 32–33 (to pur-
    chase, 188)
Collision course, right-of-way in
    (quick reference), 212–
    214
Combination (red-and-green)
    light, 180
Coming about, 118
Compass:
    compensation of, 46–47
    deviation table, 47–50
    digital read-out, 53
    drawing, 105
    gyro, 56
    handbearing (emergency),
    52–53, 88–89
    to identify shoreline, 54
    ship's (magnetic), 40–54, 85–
    87
Compass card, 41, 179

Compass degrees, 57–58 (quick reference, 200)
and danger bearing, 96–98
Compass lights, 185
Compass rose, 7–8, 26–27 (quick reference, 198, 200)
Course, plotting a, 55–73 quick reference, 200–206)
Course calculator, 10, 63
Course line, 7–10, 57–66 (quick reference, 201–202)
with current, 159
in tacking under sail, 118–119
Course over the ground (COG), 119–123
Crossing, right-of-way in (quick reference), 212
Current, tidal, 154–163

Danger bearing, 96–98
Danger whistle signal (quick reference), 212–213
Daybeacon (daymark), 13, 14, 15–16 (quick reference, 194–195)
Dead reckoning, see DR track
Deck watch, see Lookout
Depth, water (quick reference), 197
See also Sounding
Deviation:
compass, 43–46, 47–53, 86–87

Deviation (cont.)
RDF, 136–137
DFS, see Distance finding station
Diaphone, 174 (quick reference, 211)
Dinghy:
depth sounding from, 129, 130
running lights on, 180
Directional light, 23
Distance (mileage), 9–10, 30–32, 59–60, 64 (quick reference, 207)
circle of, 105–110
estimating, 80–81, 83–84
formula (distance/speed/time), 10–11, 62–63 (quick reference, 200–201)
indicator, 74–81
Distance-depth record, 127–128
Distance finding station (DFS), 140–141
Distress signals (quick reference), 215
Dividers, 9
"Dog bark" navigation, 173
DR (dead reckoning) track, 111–114, 170–171 (quick reference, 201–202)
Drawbridge, see Bridge
Drawing compass, 105
Drift of current, 154–155
estimating, 157

Ebb of current, 155

Echo sounder, 125–127
EP, *see* Estimated position
Equal-interval light, 22
Estimated position (EP), 135–136 (quick reference, 205–206)
Estimated time of arrival (ETA), 64–65
Estimating:
    course, 157–159
    current, 157
    distance, 80–81, 83–84
    speed, 80–81, 160–161
    tidal range, 168
ETA, *see* Estimated time of arrival

Fathom, 24, 25
    See also Sounding
Fix, 99–101 (quick reference, 203–205)
    by circle of distance, 105–110
    by loran, 147
    by Omega, 147–151
    by omni, 152–153
    by radar, 143–146
    running, 102–104
Fixed light, 22
Flashing light, 22
Flashlight, 180, 185, 186
Flood of current, 155
Fog, 170–177
    and plotting a course, 66, 68, 111–114, 175
    radar reflectors in, 144, 172

Fog (*cont.*)
    signals, 139–141, 171–172, 173–175 (quick reference, 210, 211)
Frequency, radio:
    distress (quick reference), 215
    Omega, 148–149, 150, 151
    omni, 152, 153
    RDF, 132–133

Geographic range, lighthouse, 18, 107–110
Gong buoy, 13, 14, 175 (quick reference, 194, 211)
Great Lakes, 168–169
    charts, 18, 24, 31–32, 35, 37–39, 59–60
    published aids (to obtain), 187–190
Great Lakes Pilot, 32–33 (to purchase, 188)
Great Lakes Rules (quick reference), 210, 212–213
Green light, 14, 15, 21, 180–183
Group lights, 23

Harbor, entering at night, 184
Harbor charts, 4, 36
Heading, ship's, 42
    in plotting a tack, 118–119
    in taking a bearing, 86–87
Height and clearance, 26, 167–168

Homing, RDF, 139, 177
Horn, 174

Inland Rules (quick reference), 208–210, 212–214
running lights, 179
International Rules (quick reference), 208–210
running lights, 179
Interpolation (to determine deviation), 50–52
Interrupted quick-flashing light, 22

Junction marker, 14–15

Knots (vs. miles per hour), 10, 60 (quick reference, 207)

Landmarks (quick reference), 196–197
Latitude, 27–32 (quick reference, 198–199)
Lead line, 129
Leeway, 119–122, 164–165
Lighthouse, 18–21, 26
fog signals, 174–175
Light List, 17–18, 19–21 (to purchase, 188–189)
for circle of distance, 107–108
for DFS, 140–141
for RDF, 132–133

Lights aboard, 178–183, 184–185
running, 178–183 (quick reference, 208–209)
Lights on navigational aids, 4, 13, 14, 15, 21–23, 183 (quick reference, 196)
Line of position (LOP), 85 (quick reference 202–203)
Local Notice to Mariners, 33–34 (to obtain, 190)
Location dot, 4, 13 (quick reference, 193)
Log book, 41, 67–69, 93, 170–171
Longitude, 27–32 (quick reference, 199)
Lookout, 139, 170, 177, 184, 185–186
LOP, *see* Line of position
Loran, 147
Lubber line, 41–42
Luminous range, 107–109

Magnetic attraction (of compass), 41–44
Magnetic compass, *see* Ship's compass
Magnetic degrees, 7–8, 55–56, 57–58, 90, 91–92 (quick reference, 200)
Marine band, RDF, 132
Marine Weather Services Charts, 141 (to purchase, 189)

Marker, *see* Buoy; Lights on navigational aids; Navigational aids
Maximum current, 155
Mean water, 24, 26, 126, 167, 168
Megaphone (in fog), 173
Memory aids:
    degrees conversion, 45
    distance/speed/time formula, 63
    navigational colors, 5, 182–183
    port and starboard, 5
    twenty-four–hour time, 61
Mercator chart projection, 31
Meridian, *see* Longitude
Midchannel marker, 15 (quick reference, 194)
Mileage, *see* Distance

National Oceanic and Atmospheric Administration (NOAA), 35
Nautical Chart Catalogs, 38–39 (to obtain, 189)
Nautical Chart Symbols and Abbreviations (Chart #1) 12 (to purchase, 189–190)
Nautical miles, 60
    See also Distance
Navigational aids, 3–6, 12–24, 174–175, 184 (quick reference, 193–197, 211)
    as a range, 16–17, 82–83

Navigational aids (*cont.*)
    See also Lights on navigational aids
Night cruising, 178–186
    circle of distance in, 105, 107–110
North Pole, 40, 41
Null, RDF, 131
    meter, 134
Nun buoy, 13 (quick reference, 193)

Oar, depth sounding with, 129–130
Occulting light, 22
Omega, 147–151
Omni (omnirange direction finding system), 152–153
Overtaking:
    right-of-way in (quick reference), 212
    whistle signal (quick reference), 213

Parallel, *see* Latitude
Parallel-lined plastic sheets, 72
Parallel rulers, 7–8, 163
Patent log, 76
Pelorus, 89–91 (quick reference, 203)
Plotting (quick reference), 200–206
    bearings, 87–88, 91–92, 96–98, 135–136

Plotting (*cont.*)
  circle of distance, 105–110
  courses, 6–11, 29–31, 55–73,
    175
  with current a factor, 157–
    163
  DR track, 111–114
  EP, 135–137
  ETA, 64–66
  fix, 99–105, 144, 147, 149–151,
    153
  instruments for, 7–8, 9, 10,
    69–72, 105, 120–121, 163
  ranges, 83
  tacks, 115–124
  See also Charts; Compass
    rose
Points (compass), 179 (quick
  reference, 200)
Polyconic chart projection, 31–
  32, 57, 59
Port side, 5, 14
  running lights on, 180, 182–
    183
Port tack, 118, 172 (quick reference, 213–214)
Powerboat:
  fog signals, 171
  right-of-way (quick refer-
    ence), 212
  running lights, 179–180
  tacking in, 115–117
  whistle signals (quick refer-
    ence), 212–213
Privileged boat (quick reference), 212, 214
Projection, chart, 31–32

Protractor:
  circular, 90–91, 120–121
  roller, 70–71
  rotatable-arm, 71–72

Quick-flashing light, 22

Radar, 143–146
  portable, 145–146
  reflectors for, 144–145, 172
Radiobeacon, 131–142 (quick
  reference, 195)
  aeronautical, 141
Radio direction finder, *see*
  RDF
Radio signals, RDF, 141
Radiotelephone, 61 (quick
  reference, 215)
Range, 16–17, 82–84 (quick
  reference, 195, 202)
RDF (radio direction finder),
  131–142 (quick reference,
  205–206)
Reciprocal:
  bearing, 87
  course, 64
Red (used for navigational
  aids), 4–7, 13–16, 21, 23
  (quick reference, 193, 194,
  195)
Red light, 13, 15, 21, 23, 180–
  183, 185
Red sector, 23
Reef, *see* Rocks
Relative bearing, 90–92
  RDF, 134–135

Rhumb line, 31
  in tacking, 116–117, 118, 119, 122–124
Right-of-way (quick reference), 212–214
Rocks, 6, 96–98
Rowboat, *see* Dinghy
Rules of the Road (to obtain), 190
  fog signals, 171–172 (quick reference, 210)
  right-of-way (quick reference), 212–214
  running lights, 178–182 (quick reference, 208–209)
  searchlight, 184
Running fix, 102–105 (quick reference, 204–205)
Running free, right-of-way when (quick reference), 213
Running lights, 178, 179–183 (quick reference, 208–209)

Sailboat:
  auxiliary, under power, *see* Powerboat
  estimating distance of, 80–81, 89
  fog signals, 171–172
  leeway, 164
  right-of-way (quick reference), 213–214
  running lights, 180

Sailboat (*cont.*)
  tacking, 118–124
SC (small craft) charts, 37
Searchlight, 184
Seconds light interval, 23
Sectional Aeronautical Charts, 141 (to purchase, 191)
Set of current, 154, 157
Sextant, 106
Ship's compass, 40–54
  bearings taken with, 85–87
  See also Compass
Ship's heading, *see* Heading, ship's
Ship's log book, *see* Log book
Short-long and Morse Code *A* light, 22–23
Signals:
  distress (quick reference), 215
  fog, 140–141, 171–172, 173–175 (quick reference, 210–211)
  whistle (quick reference), 212–213
  See also Lights on navigational aids; Navigational aids
Single line of position, *see* Line of position
Siren, 175
"Sixty D Street," 63
Slack water, 155
Small craft:
  charts, 37
  speed indicator, 77

SOG, *see* Speed over the
  ground
Sounding, 6, 24, 125–130
Sounds, *see* Signals
Speed, 9–10, 60–61, 64
  estimating, with current,
    159–160
  in fog, 171
  formula (distance/speed/
    time), 10–11, 62–63 (quick
    reference, 200–201)
  indicator, 74–81
  knots conversion in determin-
    ing (quick reference),
    207
Speed over the ground (SOG),
    158–162
Spring tide, 168
Stadimeter, 106
Starboard side, 5, 13
  running lights on, 180, 182–
    183
Starboard tack, 118, 171 (quick
    reference, 213–214)
Statute miles, 60
  See also Distance
Stern, 5
  and running lights, 179–180

Tachometer, 79
Tacking:
  powerboat, 115–117
  sailboat, 118–124
Taffrail log, 75–77
  to check leeway, 164–165
Tidal current, *see* Current

Tidal Current Charts, 156–157
  (to purchase, 191)
Tidal Current Tables, 155–156
  (to purchase, 191)
Tide, 166–169
Tide Tables, 166–168 (to pur-
  chase, 191)
Time, 10–11
  of arrival, estimated (ETA),
    64–65
  formula (distance/speed/
    time), 10–11, 62–63 (quick
    reference, 200–201)
  twenty-four–hour, 61–62
    (quick reference, 201)
Track, 158–159
  COG, 120
  DR, 111–114
Transducer, 125, 127
True degrees, 26–27, 56, 57, 90,
    157 (quick reference,
    200)
"True Virgins Conversion
  Steps," 44–46 (quick ref-
    erence, 200)
  and bearings, 86–87, 91–92
Twenty-four–hour time, 61–62
  (quick reference, 201)

Variation, compass, 27, 37, 42–
    43, 45, 53, 87
Vertical angle (to compute dis-
    tance), 106
Visibility, nighttime, 107–110,
    183–186
  See also Fog

Visibility-obstructed signal
  (quick reference), 213
VOR and VORTAC, 153

Walker log, 76
Whistle buoy, 13, 14, 175
  (quick reference, 194,
  211)
Whistle signals, right-of-way
  (quick reference), 212–
  213

White light, 13, 14, 15, 21, 179–
  182, 183
Windward boat (quick reference), 213

Zero phase difference, 149–
  151
Zigzagging in a channel, 128–
  129